The Green Room

The Green Room

A Mother's Truth

Liliane Colburn

iUniverse, Inc.
New York Lincoln Shanghai

The Green Room
A Mother's Truth

Copyright © 2005 by liliane colburn

All rights reserved. No part of this book may be used or reproduced by any means, graphic, electronic, or mechanical, including photocopying, recording, taping or by any information storage retrieval system without the written permission of the publisher except in the case of brief quotations embodied in critical articles and reviews.

iUniverse books may be ordered through booksellers or by contacting:

iUniverse
2021 Pine Lake Road, Suite 100
Lincoln, NE 68512
www.iuniverse.com
1-800-Authors (1-800-288-4677)

ISBN-13: 978-0-595-35588-4 (pbk)
ISBN-13: 978-0-595-80072-8 (ebk)
ISBN-10: 0-595-35588-9 (pbk)
ISBN-10: 0-595-80072-6 (ebk)

Printed in the United States of America

Contents

BIOGRAPHY..................................vii
FOREWORD...................................ix
THE FLEETING CAMELOT........................1
THE MAKING OF A NAVY SEAL..................11
MOVING ON..................................21
FALLING IN LOVE AGAIN......................28
THE ACCIDENT...............................44
THE SUMMER OF EL NIÑO......................66
THE RE-ENTRY...............................76
OUT OF THE GREEN ROOM......................83
DESPAIR, HOPE AND FAITH....................98
AS GOOD AS IT GETS........................116
JUMPING AGAIN.............................126
THE ENCINO MAN............................133
TRAVELS WITH MARK.........................151
LITTLE VICTORIES..........................160
DON'T YOU EVER DIE!.......................163
MY OWN WORDS-WHEN I LEFT THE GREEN ROOM...169

Biography

Liliane Colburn was born in Paris, France on October 17, 1927 and spent her teenage years during WW II in Nazi occupied France. In 1946 she arrived in the U.S. as a war bride and resided in Detroit, MI. for the next twenty five years. She had two daughters, Jacqueline and Michele with her first husband, divorced and remarried and in 1960 gave birth to her son Mark. She became a widow when she was forty, and moved to Ft. Lauderdale, FL with Mark in 1972. At the age of sixty, when Mark moved to California to pursue his dreams, Liliane moved to Petoskey, MI to be near her daughter Michele and her growing family. This is where she now resides.

In 1997, while ready to relax and enjoy her "golden years" in beautiful Petoskey, God gave her the challenge of her life. Her Navy SEAL son Mark had a parachute accident that changed her world, and his, forever. With love of family to pull her through the many heart wrenching, drama laden moments during her son's recovery, at age seventy seven, she now enjoys the glorious opportunity to tell this story. This is her first book.

Foreword

I was inspired and determined to write my son's story but I knew my English was not strong enough to express myself as I wanted to. At a local book store, I ran into a former French student I had tutored named Jacques LaMarche. He was there promoting his new book. I asked him if he would be able to take my tapes, dictating Mark's story, and put them into a book format. He accepted my offer and we started working together. Our work was on going over a period of six months when I let my daughter Michele read the first paragraph. To my surprise she was crying as she read and she started to give us more information on medical aspects. She then got very involved in editing and helped me to continue. My daughter Jacki was kind enough to give me her diary of Mark's days in the hospital. And finally Mark himself, at first a silent witness to the making of the book, slowly became more aware of the world around him, and offered meaningful input as he nudged us to finish the book. True success, is always a joint effort.

THE FLEETING CAMELOT

You may think that this is a story about television, and that the green room is someplace that you stay in until you go into the studio and appear on a TV show. This room that you may have in mind is one where they serve you a few drinks while you wait to become a celebrity; or perhaps you already are a celebrity. But there is also another green room; it's the green room of the perfect wave. For a surfer the ultimate experience is finding yourself inside the cocoon of a forceful wave. Once there, you can stay inside until the raw forces of nature thrust you back into reality and you're slapped in the face by the world you had briefly escaped. This is, in a way, what happened to my son, Mark.

When it came to Mark and his innate way of making you smile or trying to please you, you had to be interested in him from the start. He was that way as a child, and he was that way when he became a man.

I remember when I was expecting him. I was eight months into my pregnancy and I had severe cramps and pains. My husband, Allan, took me to the hospital, and as they brought me into the exam room, the nurses were laughing as they said, "This child wants to come out in the worst way." They called the doctor, who was at a formal affair, and he arrived a half-hour later, still wearing his tuxedo. Surprised, he said, "I certainly didn't expect him this month." So, instead of being born at the end of November, Mark was born on October 27th, 1960.

Since he weighed only four-and-a-half pounds, he wasn't an especially beautiful child. His chin seemed to be missing. But to my husband, he was gorgeous. Mark was his only child and a child of our love. The doctor assured me that it was natural for someone so tiny to need time to develop, and in a few weeks, Mark's little face filled up as promised and he was beautiful.

When we brought him home, Micki and Jacki—my daughters from a previous marriage—were so happy to see their baby brother. Micki, who was eight years old, said, "Oh, he's beautiful." Then Allan said, "Isn't he the most beautiful child you've ever seen?" But Micki said, "Well, the most beautiful child is Jesus Christ," which made Allan laugh because he was Jewish. I still remember how many times he told that story.

Mark loved everyone and everyone loved him. No one had seen such a smiling face. He was always in a good mood and was always moving.

I had come to America from France when I was eighteen. In Paris, I had married a GI stationed in France. After the war had ended, I followed him back to the States, and I had my two daughters, Jacqueline and Michele (whom we called Jacki and Micki). Our marriage lasted for nine years.

I married Allan when I was thirty-one and had Mark when I was thirty-two. We lived in a family-oriented subdivision called Palmer Woods Manor in Oak Park, a suburb of Detroit.

Allan was a successful businessman. We had many friends, and he was regarded as a *bon vivant*. He loved life—loved to eat, drink and smoke. He also loved my daughters and me, and he adored his son.

THE FLEETING CAMELOT

Marky (as we called him then) decided at the age of three that he was going to dress and act like Superman, and I think he was Superman until he was ten. Each year we had to get him a bigger Superman suit. When he grew out of one, my sister in New York would send us another, and Marky would run through the neighborhood with his cape flying behind him. If he lost it, I'd give him my Hermes scarf, and off he'd go again.

By the age of four, he already had a sense of adventure. One day, for example, he decided to get on the school bus that stopped near our house every morning. We looked everywhere for him until a woman from the school called and said that they had an extra little boy who was dressed in a Superman suit. When we went to get him, we asked him what in the world he was doing. He said that his friends from across the street were going to school, so he thought he'd see what it was like. From that day on, everyone in the neighborhood, as well as his sisters' friends, always referred to him as Superman.

When Mark went to school at the age of five, his teacher told us that he should repeat kindergarten because his attention span was short. I didn't listen, because I was afraid his feelings would be hurt if he didn't go into the first grade with his friends. However, the first grade teacher told me that Mark talked all the time and that he was all over the room. She thought that he was "hyperkinetic" and should be tested.

Very few people, including us, had heard of that and I was very upset. But Allan thought we should have the tests done, so we took Mark to Children's Hospital in Detroit and had him tested. After an hour, the chief of psychiatry said that he was hyperkinetic and suggested we give him Ritalin.

The doctor said, "It's not so bad. With one pill in the morning and one after lunch, he'll be able to do his schoolwork and control his energy. Didn't you ever notice that he was always into everything at home?" "No," I said. "He's always happy, and he makes everyone else happy. Sure, it's hard to take him to a restaurant, because he does his puffy-cheeked imitation of Alfred Hitchcock or goes over to strangers' tables and asks them questions. But he's so funny that everyone laughs." The doctor laughed and said, "Yes, he's very smart and will probably be a comedian someday. However, he should probably take the Ritalin until puberty. Most children outgrow the need for it by then, but for now he needs to give his attention to his schoolwork."

We hated to have him take the medication, and never had him take it on the weekend, but his schoolwork did improve.

THE FLEETING CAMELOT

On Saturdays, Allan—who was not a sportsman—would take Marky to the Sydney Hills club to swim. In the summer, they swam in the outdoor pool, and in the winter and spring, they swam indoors.

Our house was always full of young people: Jacki's high school friends, Micki's middle school friends—and Marky would be running around amongst all of them. At times, Allan and I had to take refuge in our bedroom.

By eight o'clock, however, Marky would be sound asleep. I still can see him watching TV in his dad's leather chair wearing his pajamas and his little John-John Kennedy haircut, snug in his father's arms. Allan was wearing what he called his "monkey suit," a one-piece lounging suit that zipped in front. I had bought him the leather chair, which was big and comfortable—just the right size for him and his little boy. They would sit together and watch "Laugh In" and "Star Trek."

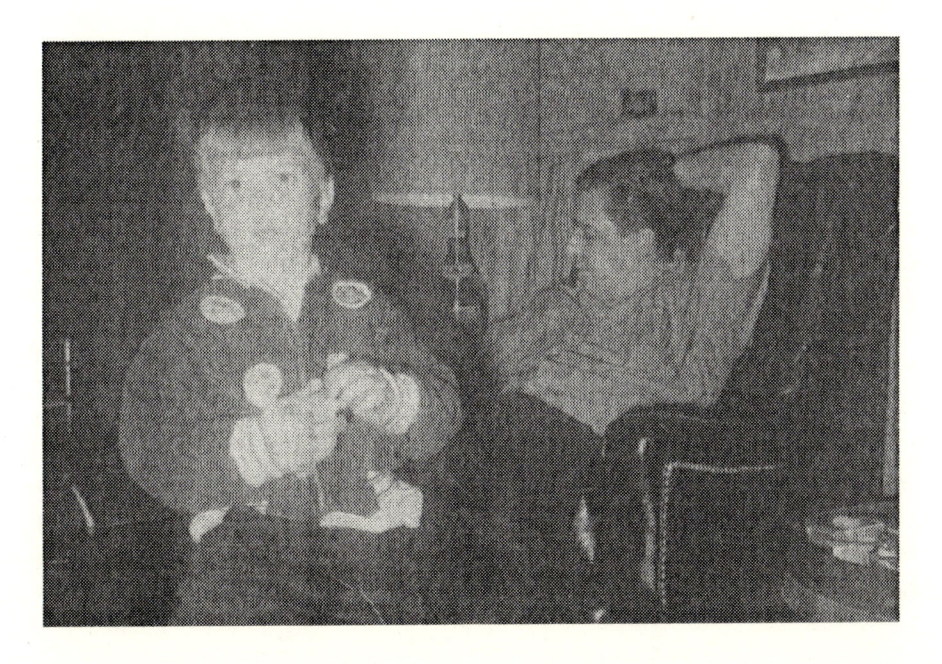

In those days, "The Graduate" was on the big screen, Elvis was king and the Beatles were on the Ed Sullivan Show. Oleg Cassini was the fashion designer of the moment, Sassoon did everybody's hair, and short skirts and white boots were everywhere. Our Frigidaire was filled with red meat, sodas and Twinkies. And we were always afraid that Jacki would bring home a long-haired "beatnik."

Jacki and Micki went to jazz dance classes, Micki was a cheerleader and Marky was still—and always—Superman, and was still doing his imitations. He would do "Mighty Mouse" and run and jump throughout the house shouting, "Here I come to save the day!"

Allan had high blood pressure, but his doctor said it wasn't bad. He told him to lose some weight and gave him some pills. Allan didn't take the pills, but he did lose some weight. I had trouble with my right kidney, and after Mark was born, I'd had to take several trips to the hospital because of it. I also had hernias on my left side, and when I told the doctor that Allan and I loved to do the "Twist," he laughed and said, "No wonder." Between the cesareans I'd had and the Twist, I guess my hernias were inevitable.

In late 1967, I turned forty and we decided to take the whole family on a vacation for Christmas, along with some of our friends and their children. So we boarded a plane and went to Curacao, where we stayed in a beautiful hotel on the beach. The girls loved it—especially having all their friends there with them. And the first thing Mark did when we weren't looking was call room service and order twenty Cokes. We all got tan and went gambling, then went shopping with the winnings. Allan bought me a cocktail ring with a burst of diamonds.

We came back on New Year's Eve. I remember that we were in a cab when midnight struck—just Allan, myself and the children. And I remember thinking that it was the best New Year's I'd ever had. I didn't know then that a month later our lives would change forever.

One late night in February, I had a lot of pain on my right side. I was upset because I didn't want to go to the hospital. My mother was visiting from France, which added to the reasons I didn't want to go. But Allan called the doctor, who said to bring me in, and told him that it sounded like a kidney stone.

Allan hated to drive when he was upset, but he took me anyhow because his twin brother, who lived across the street, couldn't come. I remember telling him in the car that everything would be okay and that I wouldn't have to go to the hospital again. I was holding his big, strong hand. It was warm and I felt reassured.

We went to the emergency room at Ford Hospital. After they took an x-ray, they told us that they wanted to keep me because they saw an internal obstruction. When I told Allan that he looked tired and should go home, he said he had heartburn, and when I told him to have the doctor have a look at him, he said, "No, it's probably the damn cigarettes. I'm probably rotten from here to here," (pointing to his chest). Bending down to kiss me, he whispered, "I could make love to you right here on the gurney." I laughed and he told me he'd be back in the morning.

Because of the IV in my arm, I twisted and turned all night. When the nurse came in at dawn, I told her that my side hurt. She told me that the doctor would be in soon to see me.

Sometime in the early morning, the doctor came in with a syringe in his hand and I remember thinking, *good, it won't hurt anymore.* But to my surprise, my sister-in-law Sharon followed him into the room and she was crying. The doctor looked at me soberly, and said, "I have some bad news." I thought, *I have cancer.* But then he said, "There is no other way but to come out and tell you. Your husband is dead."

I couldn't comprehend and looked at Sharon, who was still sobbing. I screamed and said, "Don't say that!" *Oh my God!* I thought. *It's my fault. He had an accident on the way home.*

"He had a massive heart attack," the doctor told me. "He died instantly."

Allan was only thirty-seven.

I pulled the IV needle out of my arm and jumped out of bed to go see him. The doctor wanted to give me a shot, but I said, "No. Give me my clothes. I want to go see him. I want to see my kids." I had the sensation that I was not myself anymore—that I was someone else watching me go through this horror from afar. I don't remember getting in the car with Sharon, but I do remember getting to the house.

Allan's brothers were there, but I could only see Micki and Mark. Jacki was away at college and was already on her way home. People were crying and my mother was hysterical. Then I heard a voice that I will never forget. "Is this the bereaved widow?" It was the man from the funeral home and I hated him for daring to call me a widow. I hated his unfamiliar, insincere voice and his cliché phrases. And I particularly hated him for saying that Allan was already at the funeral home and that I could only see him after five p.m.

Micki told me what had happened. Allan had come home and told my mother that I was okay. Then he fixed himself a snifter of Courvoisier and put it on the dresser, took off his shirt and pants and, dressed in just his shorts and undershirt, fell to the floor, and died. The door was closed and no one had heard his fall.

At seven-thirty, Mark went into the room. He was surprised to see his dad sleeping on the floor, but gave him a good-bye kiss before he went to school. A little while after that, Allan's twin brother, Merton, called and wanted to talk to him. Micki went into his bedroom and saw him there, so she ran back to the phone and told Merton that Allan was on the floor, that he wasn't moving and that he was cold. Merton ran over in his underwear and began CPR, but it was too late.

I saw him at the funeral home. He was not Allan anymore. They told me not to touch him, but I did anyway. I wanted to warm him up and hold him against my heart. He was beautiful, in spite of the awful funeral-home makeup they'd put on him. I was searching for his usual scent. He was like a wax figure of the man I loved. I put his wedding ring on his finger and tucked pictures of the two of us and the children in the pocket of the suit that his brother had chosen for his burial.

When I came home, I called the same psychologist that had taken care of Mark, and told him what had happened. "What do I do?" I asked him. "Do I take Mark to see his father being buried?" He told me that I should, and added that after everything was finished, I should have Mark come and see him. My poor little seven-year-old had found his dad on the floor, and hadn't known that he was dead. I couldn't imagine how this memory might affect him in the future.

Two thousand people came to Allan's funeral. Everyone loved him. He was a good man and a good friend to all. He had black friends and white friends. Some were rich and some were poor. Some were Jewish and others belonged to many different denominations. There were waitresses, bartenders, musicians, entertainers, a former governor—even people from the underworld.

Allan had never denied himself or anyone else the good life. Living life to the fullest was his style, and he had lived as though he knew he was going to die young.

At the funeral, Marky shook the open coffin and said, "That's enough! Dad, wake up!" Micki cried quietly. Jacki was so hysterical that you could hear her sobs throughout the funeral home. My sister, whom I adored, was frightened. She didn't want to look at his body. I told her that Allan was my father, my child, my friend, my love, and that I wanted her to see him for my sake. But it scared her and, as time passed, I always regretted that I had asked that of her.

It was cold when they put him in the earth. I held my kids in my fur coat and—in that eerie out-of-body sensation—I watched myself look at him for the last time, in that shiny, black box. His death marked the end of my Camelot.

When we came home from the funeral, Marky asked me, "Mom, are you going to die, too? I don't want to be an orphan." I took him by the shoulders and said, "No! I will never die! I promise you." And I think he believed me. In fact, I think he still does. "Not only will I never die," I said, "but you won't either. I went through World War II and I didn't die, because I'm a survivor. And you're going to be a survivor, too. As long as you need me I will be here." I didn't know it at the time, but I was teaching my children during those difficult days, to survive, no matter what happens.

Allan's death changed our lives forever. I am now seventy-four, and not a day passes that I don't think of him. No matter what I do, no matter where I go, he is with me. He remains—and always will be—my only love. Our songs are still playing, our family still tells the same jokes, and I always think of that part of my life with love and tenderness.

Life went on, however, and I still had to take care of my kids. After struggling with my pain and my life and money, I recreated myself when Micki went to college. Eventually, I moved to New York with Mark and stayed there for a year. Jacki had finished college and moved to Troy, Michigan, where she was teaching elementary school. My sister and her husband were in New York, along with her daughter, son-in-law and two grandchildren: Caroline and Christopher. I enrolled Mark at Buckley, a private school in Manhattan, and started to make sense of my life—for Mark's sake as well as my own.

At first, New York was fun. My mother, who had recently moved to America, had a small apartment in Manhattan and I had a big one near the East River. Every weekend Mark and I went to lunch at my sister's on our bikes, and then to Central Park. Sometimes we'd go to a movie instead, or take in a show like, *Hair*,

Jesus Christ Superstar, Fiddler on the Roof, or whatever happened to be hot at the time.

Mark wore a suit and tie to school. He'd catch the bus from the front of our apartment and come home at three-thirty. After school, he sometimes went on outings with Caroline and Christopher.

One morning, we were in the elevator and I looked at him and thought that he looked like a thirty-year-old man in his suit and tie, carrying his valise. Outside of school, he was never with kids his age, and when my niece decided to move back to France with her children, I came to the conclusion that New York wasn't a good situation for him. So, during the time he was at Camp Walden in Michigan, the camp he had gone to each summer, I called and told him that we were moving to Fort Lauderdale, Florida. He was all for it. His father and I had always had great vacations there, I knew Mark would love the ocean, and the girls would have an interesting place to visit. All I had was ten-thousand dollars from the sale of our house to use as a down payment, a six-hundred dollar Social Security payment for being a widow with a child, and five-hundred per month from a trust fund.

THE MAKING OF A NAVY SEAL

We moved to Florida in 1972. Mark was going to be twelve in October and I was about to turn forty-four. Our new house was in Pompano Beach, about ten miles north of Fort Lauderdale. By getting slightly out of the city, I was able to find a place that was reasonably priced. It had a pool and was on a canal, where I could have a speedboat and go just about anywhere via the inland waterway. Mark was thrilled about it, and as a joke, he'd say, "When I came back from camp, my mother had moved away."

I went back to Michigan to pick him up. I was so proud of him: he had swum across the lake at camp, learned to ride a horse, and been in a play. He'd also been in a play at Buckley, where he played a dog and had done such a good job that he was the talk of the school.

When we were still in New York, he had begged me to get him a unicycle. At first I said, "no", but he persisted and assured me that he could teach himself to ride. It was hard for me to refuse him of anything he wanted because I felt bad that he had to grow up without a dad. I thought how a father would allow him to do some of these daring things, so I bought the unicycle. Knowing his love for challenges, I had no doubt that he would be able to do it. He hadn't had much of a chance to practice it on the busy Manhattan streets, but as soon as we got to Florida, he began to ride it on the street in front of our house. And, sure enough, before too long, he had mastered it.

The school system in Fort Lauderdale had a poor reputation at that time, and the same was true for Pompano Beach. When I voiced my concerns to the realtor, he suggested Westminster Academy, the Presbyterian school that his son attended. I checked up on it and heard good things: small classes, no drugs and wonderful supervision, and even though we weren't Presbyterian, they didn't mind having Mark as long as he followed their rules.

I had become a Catholic when I was still in France, right after it was liberated. It was the religion of my mother's side of the family, and when I was left with her sister for two years, I had begun to go to church with her. I believed in God and all the saints, and when I turned sixteen, I decided to get baptized and make my first communion. But perhaps since Mark's father was Jewish, we had reached the point early on in our marriage where neither of us practiced our faiths. As a consequence, I thought the Presbyterian school would be a good opportunity for Mark to learn something about religion. I wanted him to have faith, because when I was growing up and things weren't going well it had always helped me.

Mark, as I had to call him then (no more Marky), had to wear a uniform consisting of a white shirt and navy pants. Since the school was two miles from our house, he'd ride there every day on his unicycle. Most of the kids in our neighborhood were boys between the ages of eight and fourteen. At first, Mark wasn't too popular, partly because he was short for his age, but also because his sense of humor tended to be at the expense of others. Also, the other kids thought that Mark felt superior to them because of his Manhattan experiences such as attending Broadway plays and eating oysters and escargot. Sometimes the other kids didn't believe him, and he came home often with a bloody nose.

After a while, I became concerned. I was going to talk to the kids but Mark told me he'd handle it himself. However, one day, a friend of mine saw how troubled I was and suggested I have Mark take karate lessons. Martial arts were just becoming popular and he assured me it would give him self confidence. It was right at the time when the first Bruce Lee movies were coming out. My sister called from New York and said I should take Mark to see one. I did, and he loved it.

So at the age of twelve, Mark stopped being Superman and became Bruce Lee. He worked on all the moves—the kicks and the punches—and karate became his life. I thought it was funny to see my baby-faced boy assume fierce facial expressions and attack poses. The fact that I didn't get hurt from his practicing so close to my face was a miracle.

Soon, he'd gained the respect of the other kids in the neighborhood, and in the fall of 1972, he joined the football team. I used to cringe when I went to see him play because he was so small. I held my breath every time all those big kids toppled over on him.

Meanwhile, I sold the diamond cocktail ring that Allan had given me and bought a motorboat. It was nice to have access to the canal from our backyard. Whenever Mark wasn't in school, we'd hop in the boat and go fishing, or find a place for a nice picnic, or connect with the Fort Lauderdale canal and eat at one of the outdoor restaurants along its banks. I was trying to do some of the things a father would do; not that he ever seemed aware that his life was different than it would have been with a dad. He was always a happy kid with a great smile, always joking and making me and everyone else laugh.

In the early seventies, a new sport arrived on the neighborhood scene, and with it came an atmosphere of competition, to see who could be the best and the most daring. Skateboarding was the most difficult of Mark's passions for me to handle because I knew he could get hurt—and he did. He would skateboard in empty swimming pools with the other kids until they were noticed by the owners and sent on their way. At other times, they'd make ramps out of lumber that had been set out in the yards of houses that were under construction. They did this until the owners noticed their supplies missing and called the police. A couple of times, the police even found the kids and made them take their ramps apart and return the wood. As a result of the skateboarding, we made several trips to the emergency room for broken ankles and wrists. Nonetheless, Mark's fearless pursuit of being the best was already obvious to me.

Mark met the boy who was to become his best friend at Westminster Academy. He and Bill Devitt had the same love of adventure and mischief, and they were always competing to see who would do the most outrageous thing. Bill learned how to ride a unicycle, too, and soon Mark had started a unicycle fad at the academy. All the boys began riding them to school and their pictures even appeared in the Fort Lauderdale News.

One day a neighbor was taking his son surfing and asked Mark, who was thirteen at the time, if he wanted to go with them. Of course he did. And his very first time on the waves, he found a new love. After that, he'd go to the ocean every chance he could. At that point, he was skateboarding, surfing, and taking karate. He wanted to take guitar lessons, too, but we talked about it and decided he really didn't have the time, so they were postponed. Life was very busy for both of us.

Westminster Academy turned out to be very strict and paddled kids when they misbehaved. They would bring the student before a panel of teachers to decide if the perpetrator deserved to be disciplined or not. The first paddling Mark got was for pulling a chair out from under a girl as she was about to sit down. I allowed it because I thought he deserved to be disciplined.

The second time he was paddled, I saw him in the morning before he left for school. His pants were huge in the back because he was wearing five pairs of underwear and an extra pair of pants. When he was about to be paddled, he came running home from school. I went back with him and asked what had happened. They told me he was to be paddled because he and Bill were late for class. I objected, saying that wasn't a good enough reason for them to hit my child. Though they agreed, I discovered later that they had paddled him anyway after I left. I had never hit my children for any reason—I never believed in it—and I wasn't about to let a stranger hit Mark. So I decided to pull him out of Westminster Academy.

At this time, Jacki was teaching in Florida and Michele was attending Michigan State University, where she met a boy and fell in love. She and Dan were a handsome couple. When Michele moved to Florida, Dan came with her. The two of them would come to the house, sometimes with a lot of friends, and it was always a joy to see them.

During this time, my mother, Nenene, was diagnosed with myasthenia gravis, a disease that attacked the muscles in her neck and chest, making it difficult to swallow food and breathe normally. She needed to have someone to check in on her. My sister in New York was not in good health, either. We all decided it would be easier if Nenene came to Florida where I could look after her, and my mother seemed to be happy with that arrangement. She had already decided that she didn't want to go back to France. She wanted to stay in America. Furthermore, she had been coming to Florida on vacation twice a year with my sister and her husband, and she always enjoyed the time she spent here.

So I found her a little apartment close to our house. She had to have a tracheotomy to help her breathe, and we found a nurse to stay with her. I went to see her every day; sometimes with Mark and sometimes with Jacki. When Michele came to visit, I'd go with her, too.

Unfortunately, I wasn't with my mother when she died. I had left her place and went to run some errands, and when I got back, she wasn't at her apartment. I called the hospital and they told me to come over right away. Mark was with me and the two of us rushed there, but she had already passed away. It made me very sad. Someone once reminded me that most people die alone, and I knew it was true. Allan had also died alone. If you can be there for someone, it's wonderful, but I knew it didn't always happen that way.

I had always thought that I would never lose my mother, even when she was very sick, but myasthenia gravis is a terrible disease and there were many times when she wanted to die. A year after she passed away, I was watching the Jerry Lewis telethon and was pleased to see that they were raising money to find a cure for the dreadful disease that had claimed her life.

According to her wishes, my three children, my sister and her husband and I buried her on American soil in Fort Lauderdale, Florida.

A few years later, my sister Jacqueline, in New York, was operated on by Michael DeBakey. She had an obstructed aorta and Dr. DeBakey, who was doing some incredible work at the time, replaced it with an artificial one. This cutting-edge technique saved her life, but her health was never the same again. She had headaches so severe that she would stay in her room for three days at a time.

In between those horrible headaches, she was still the wonderful sister I loved. She was also my friend and had always been like a mother to me, and a beautiful woman who, although eight years older than I, looked like my younger sister.

In March of 1978, my daughter Jacki gave birth to a beautiful baby boy named Nicholas. A week later, Michele and Dan were married in Fort Lauderdale on a yacht a friend had loaned us for the occasion. Mark had fractured his ankle and it had been put in a cast. He didn't want to wear a cast to the wedding, and he was determined to take it off. This was hardly a challenge for Mark. He put his leg in the pool for at least an hour, until the plaster melted off. He went to the wedding wearing just a small ace wrap.

The day my daughter got married was probably the happiest I'd been since Allan died. I loved my new son-in-law and felt that things were going to be great. Everyone was healthy and happy. Life was good for me and my family for the next few years. And then, as so often happened in our lives, we had another loss.

It was 1981 when I got the call from my nephew in New York. He told me that my sister had died during the night. I thanked God that both my daughters were with me at the time, Jacki with Nicholas, and Michele with her first baby, Daniel. I left for New York so I could see my sister before she was flown back to Paris for her burial. She had always wanted to be buried in France.

The loss of my sister, mother and husband was a lot for me to bear. Jacqueline had been everything a sister could be, and there was never any competition or jealousy between us—just love and understanding. I felt so very grateful to have my children. My biggest fear became losing one of them. After you lose people you love, those that you still have become more precious than ever. I thought that losing one of my kids would be more than I could endure, and I thanked God that they were all healthy. I also realized that I had to hide my fears for their sake.

To make things worse, I was being tested by the things Mark was doing. If there was a hurricane in Florida, he'd drop everything and search for the ultimate wave, the longest ride inside a perfect tunnel of green and blue sea, or, the green room. I'd often get calls from school saying he was absent, only to see a picture of him storm surfing, in the next day's paper. I'd known what he was up to anyway. He'd go surfing and park his car anywhere he could, whether it was legal or not. So storm surfing and parking tickets went hand in hand.

During high school and college, Mark had had a variety of jobs, but they never lasted long because he became bored quickly and always wanted to move on to something new. However, the jobs he had were always interesting. Once he was employed to put advertising balloons onto the roofs of businesses. Another time, acting as someone called a "hooker," he was attached to a helicopter and used a hook to drop off and pick up bags of checks from the roofs of various banks, transferring them from one to another, a procedure that expedited the check-clearing process before the days of computers. Though Mark loved this job, he eventually had to quit because the safety harness that was attached to him hurt his side. After that, he had a brief stint as a carpet installer, and then went to work as a karate instructor. That job was his favorite, but the owner of the school where he taught was going broke, and every time he paid Mark, the check bounced.

During that time he had fallen in love with a beautiful girl named Patty. I loved Patty. She and Mark were both twenty, but neither of them was mature enough to get married. After nearly four years, their relationship began to fizzle and Mark began to dream about going to California.

Meanwhile, he had rekindled his interest in the guitar and taught himself to play. At first it was a chore to listen to him because he wasn't very good, but gradually he improved. In a short time he was a fairly accomplished guitar player and formed a band with some friends. They would come to my house and practice because none of the other parents would let them play in their homes.

The band practiced nearly every day and they set their sights on hitting it big. Unfortunately, it's not easy to hit the big time, and they soon learned this harsh reality. They had a few gigs in Fort Lauderdale, but it was never enough to make a living.

In the meantime, Mark taught himself to play the piano and wrote and sang his own songs. When his best friend, Bill, went into the Marines to become a pilot, Mark lamented his departure with his song, *My Friend Bill Went into the Marines*. At one of Mark's club gigs, a local DJ heard him and invited him to be on his radio show. During the interview he was able to sing the song he wrote about Bill.

18   The Green Room

THE MAKING OF A NAVY SEAL 19

In 1982, he was invited by my nephew in France, who was a promoter, to work as a roadie for the Rolling Stones. Mark jumped at the opportunity. He was introduced to the band in Nice, at a restaurant that had once been a castle. When he met Mick Jagger, he became so star struck that he lost his balance, falling into Keith Richard's lap and prompting the whole band to laugh at him. Another time, as thousands of fans were waiting for the Stones to begin their concert, Mark went onstage with his guitar, to the cheers of a crowd that thought he was Mick Jagger. To this day, he talks about traveling with the Stones throughout France.

After Bill came back from the service, he went to California. Mark wanted to live there, too. He even went to San Diego to check it out, but came back because he missed Patty. When he returned, he got a good job with Ford in the credit department. They told him that they would transfer him to California after a while.

His departure for California was quintessential Mark in style. He had an old car, so badly beaten up that I used to ask him not to park it in front of the house. Later, a friend of mine told me that when Mark left for the airport to go to California, he tossed the car keys to the valet who was helping him with his luggage and said, "Here's your tip, dude. Catch the keys. I'm off to California to look for the green room."

Mark could always make everybody laugh, including me, and the house seemed empty when he left. But I was happy for him and glad that he was finally on his way. He had a good job and, somewhere along the line, I knew that he would become a man.

MOVING ON

Mark called me every week from California. He and Michele, who was living in Colorado, were good about keeping in touch. Jacki had lived near me for eight years and we saw each other often. I had also kept in touch with my sister's daughter, Daniele, who was back in France. She was very dear to me and I went to see her every two years. At the same time, I would see my brother Jacques, who had never moved from France, along with his wife Liliane and daughter Pascal. He was a unique character and a true Frenchman, who had been part of the underground resistance during World War II and refused to learn English. I loved to ask him questions about our past, as I was the youngest in the family and a lot had happened that I didn't remember or fully appreciate. So he told me everything I wanted to know.

When Mark left home, I decided to get a job. Nicholas was already in school, so I only had to baby-sit on weekends, and I knew I couldn't just stay home and do nothing. So I went to work for a dress shop that sold designer clothes—Chanel, Dior, and many other French designers—and I enjoyed the job.

Whenever I heard from Mark, I would ask him about his work with Ford. It was a good job, but I was always afraid he wouldn't stick with it. He liked various aspects of it, like being a "repo" man and picking up cars when people didn't make their payments. However, I knew that most of the job had him on a computer from nine to five, and I couldn't see him doing that for too long. Still, it lasted a year and he made some good friends, with whom he shared an apartment. Even after he moved on, he kept in touch with them. Once someone was Mark's friend, he or she was a friend for life.

In 1989, Michele and Dan had talked to me about moving back to Michigan. They had moved to Petoskey, a quaint little town in the northwest part of the Lower Peninsula, they wanted to raise their family there. They already had three boys, and Michele was expecting their fourth. She also wanted to finish her master's thesis in nursing. After being a hospital nurse for ten years, she had decided to go back to school to become an advanced practice nurse, and she thought if I could watch the children—especially the baby—while she was finishing school, it would help her a lot. I thought about how I wouldn't have to work anymore, and would be busy and happy in that little resort town in Northern Michigan.

So I put my dog in the car and drove from Florida to Petoskey, Michigan. Michele and Dan helped me get a wonderful house in a beautiful neighborhood and I helped take care of their children. Their school was nearby, and their house was not far from mine, so it was convenient. I picked the kids up after school and Michele would come get them when she finished work.

Meanwhile, out in California, Mark had met a girl and was very much in love. He had even brought her to Michigan for me to meet, and I believe he thought she was the one. We thought she was a lovely person and not long after I met her, Mark told me that they had made arrangements to get married. However, he was thinking of leaving Ford and becoming a Navy SEAL.

He told me that he was apprehensive about joining the navy, though, because there was no assurance that he'd become a SEAL. And if he couldn't be one, he had no desire to join up. If he did enlist, it was a chance he'd have to take. He'd have to go through boot camp first, and if he didn't make it through the SEAL training, he'd be stuck in the navy for four years.

I urged him to tell his girlfriend about his intentions before they got too far into their engagement. At first he didn't have the heart to tell her that he might be joining the navy, but I sensed that it might make a big difference. When he finally told her, her parents got very angry because they felt Mark would never be home with her. Soon, the engagement ended. I knew he loved her, but she gave him back her ring, and at the age of twenty-eight, Mark joined the navy.

Though I never doubted he could do it, I was very worried about Mark because I knew how disappointed he'd be if he wasn't accepted into the SEAL program. When he graduated from boot camp, I went to see him in Coronado, California. Bill and another friend, Lew, who was already a SEAL, were there, giving him advice and telling him what he'd be up against.

Just before I left California, the navy accepted Mark to BUDS training, (Basic Underwater Demolition School). Bill and Lew took us out to diner to celebrate, and as we ate I learned a bit more about what was involved. I was told that Mark would have to endure "hell week," during which he'd go through the most strenuous training anyone could bear. At the time, I could never have imagined how rough it was going to be. I'd never seen a film of it or had any real knowledge of this kind of training. I'd only heard that the SEALs were an elite part of the navy and that they were very secretive about their missions.

As a mother, of course I was worried, but I knew that when Mark wanted to do something—especially if he wanted to *prove* that he could do something—there was nothing I could say or do to talk him out of it. Still, I couldn't believe that my little boy, the same little boy I'd taken out of school because I was afraid they were going to paddle him, was going to go through that rigid training.

A movie called *Navy SEALs* had just come out and Bill suggested that I see it, although Lew said that it didn't depict the training accurately. However, when I went to see the film, I realized that Mark was going to go through something special.

Mark told me that only ten percent of those trying to become SEALs made it through BUDS and hell week. He also informed us that he couldn't talk to anyone until hell week was over, but that if he made it through, we could come to the completion ceremony. I was hoping so much that he would make it because he wanted it so badly. He was so proud when he told me what an honor it was to be a SEAL, and I knew it would be hard on him if he wasn't accepted.

I was settled in Petoskey when Mark called with the fantastic news. He was a Navy SEAL. Michele and Jacki came to California with me for the induction ceremony and they were as proud of him as I was. They had always been such an influence on their little brother's life and had loved their stepfather, so, just like me, they thought of how wonderful it would've been for Allan to see his son then.

The ceremony in Coronado was wonderful. Each graduating SEAL, in his uniform, was congratulated by his commanders and each officer, one by one. This was followed by a small party where everybody could congratulate each other. Afterwards, we went out to lunch with Bill and Lew, and I was so proud. We took a lot of pictures. It was a great day for all of us.

I asked Mark, "Are you done with your training," and he said, "Oh, no! Now the real training starts and it'll be a year before I finish and get my trident, but the training is *never* over. A trident is a pin that only SEALs could wear and you only got it when you had completed your yearlong training. I asked if there was still a chance that he wouldn't become a SEAL, but he said that he'd gone through the worst part and it would be hard to get bumped from the program. Still, he told me that the training would always be very demanding and now it was part of his job.

So Michele and I returned to Michigan and Mark began his training. I only heard from him two or three times a month. Although he could never tell me where he was, he'd call and tell me he was alright. During that time, probably four or five months after beginning his training, Desert Storm began and I didn't hear from him for a long time. Many times I called the number he had left for me and somebody would check and say that he was okay, but I never knew where he was during the entire time the war lasted, and I still don't know.

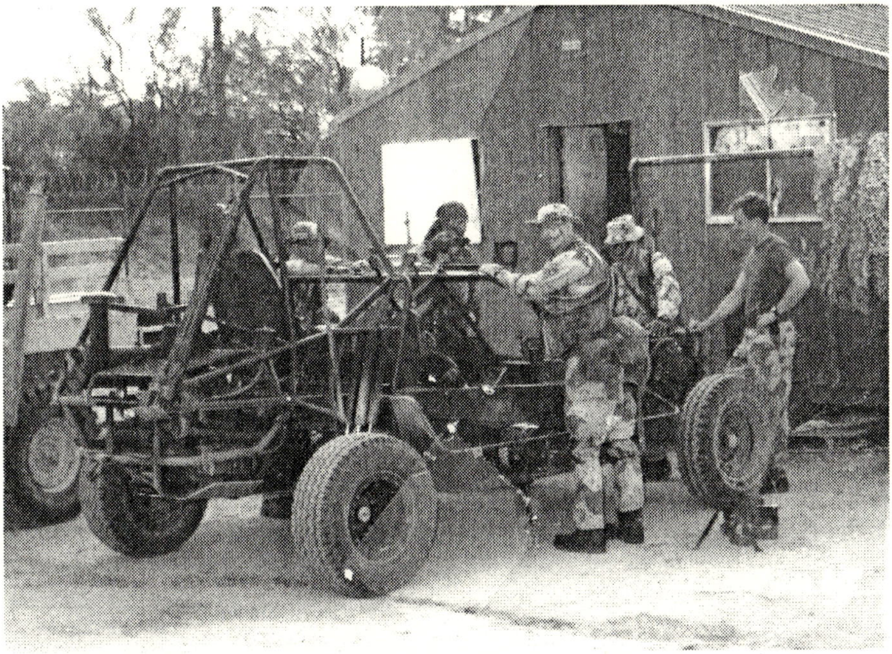

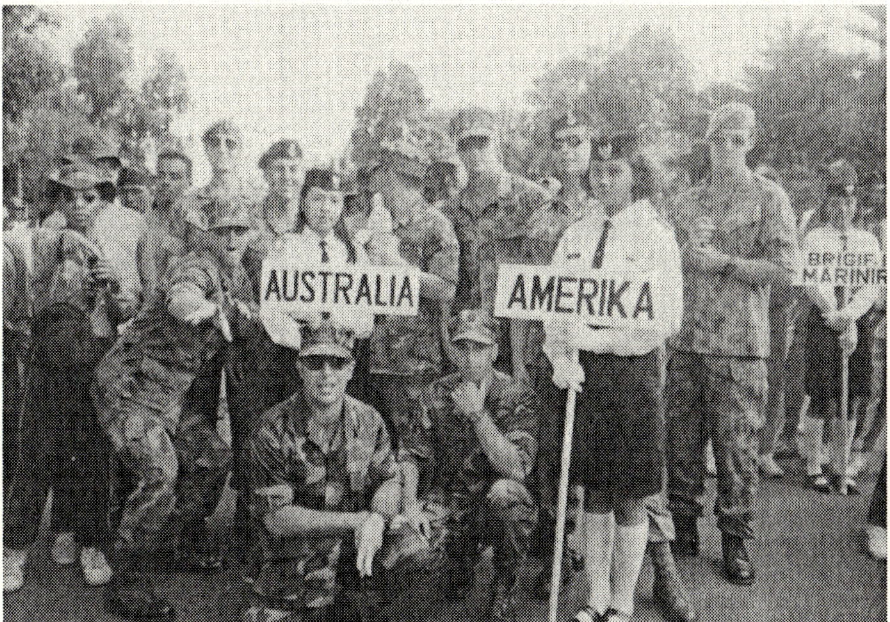
AUSTRALIA
AMERIKA

26   The Green Room

MOVING ON   27

Photo shoot for Forbes magazine article about "teams"

FALLING IN LOVE AGAIN

Time went by and Desert Storm ended. Then Mark was deployed at different locations for six months at a time. Sometimes he would call in the middle of a six-month period, and sometimes he couldn't, but I knew that he would as soon as it was possible. It was such a pleasure to hear his voice, and I could tell that he was as content as he'd ever been. He was doing something that he wanted to do and he was proud of himself.

During that time, he had also met a girl, a paralegal who worked for a lawyer in San Diego. The two had fallen in love, and one Christmas, to our joy, he brought Tania up to Michigan. We had a wonderful time. Michele and Dan and their four children were at the house, and Jacki Nicholas came up from Florida. Mark and his girlfriend stayed with us through New Year's, and it was great to have all three of my kid's home for the holidays. We were all happy for Mark and thought that things were serious between him and Tania. By that time, they had been together for about a year and a half, and we thought that she might be the one he would marry. But he wasn't ready to make a commitment.

A short time later, Tania's sister got married and Mark went with her to the wedding. He called and told me how lovely her family was, which gave me even more reason to believe that something would come of his relationship with her. But soon after, in 1995, he was sent on another six-month deployment.

Whenever he was based in Guam, he called often but never thought about the time difference. He would sometimes call Michele in the middle of the night and wake her up, only to wonder why she didn't sound more excited to hear from him. She was always glad to talk to him, but would say, "Gee, I wish you'd call when I'm awake." Then, he would often call me. Mark knew that I was always glad to talk to him, regardless of the time of night.

Once he called and told me he had been going out for a week with a girl that he'd met and really liked. I was surprised because Tania was waiting for him back in California. So I asked him about that and Mark admitted that he'd have to explain the situation to her. He told me the new girl was in the navy, too, and that they'd really hit it off. I didn't think it would last, but about three or four weeks later, he called again and said, "Mom, Eva's pregnant and I think I'm going to marry her."

I didn't know what to think. It was a lot to take in. I asked him if he was sure and he said he was. Then I asked him if he had told Tania and he said he still needed to do that. I told him it would break her heart. He said he knew that and felt terrible about the way things had turned out, but he hoped she would understand.

When it came to love, I never told my kids what to do because I felt they had to make their own choices and live with them. But this time I wasn't so sure. I wanted to have a grandchild and I wanted Mark to have a baby, but I was skeptical about the situation. However, Mark seemed to know what he wanted and nothing I said would've made a difference anyway once he had his mind set. Still, I was worried for him.

About a month later, he called me to say, "Guess what? Eva had a test and the doctor said we're going to have twins, twin boys." He was thrilled and said, "This is so wonderful! Can you imagine me having twins?" Mark told me that when he finished his deployment, Eva would leave the navy and they would get married. I was very happy for him because he seemed happy and I knew he had always wanted to have children.

As he was leaving Guam, Mark called me from his plane. He told me that Eva was at the apartment they had been sharing, and I told him I wanted to talk to her. I called and introduced myself and said I had heard the news about the twins and that I was so happy for her and Mark. I asked when they were getting married and she said they'd be married when they got back to California.

Mark had said that having his own twins was like a gift, especially after having lost his father at such a young age. He sounded really happy, and whenever one of my kids is happy, I am too, even though I knew they would have a lot of difficulties ahead of them. But I'm an old romantic and I always believed that love conquers everything.

Then Tania called me from California and I could tell that Mark hadn't broken the news to her yet. I felt terrible because she was a lovely girl and I knew how crushed she'd be. She said she felt like something was wrong, though she didn't know what it was. And I couldn't tell her. She told me that Mark had seemed really cold and that he had said he wanted to talk to her when he got back from Guam. I tried my best to say the right words, hinting that maybe she should let it go for a little while. But then she went on to tell me that he seemed distant when he went on deployment, but that everything had always gone back to normal when he got home.

As I listened to her, I felt heartbroken. And after I hung up, I thought about men in general, including my son, and how they were all the same and could leave you in a minute. I also figured this new girl had to be something special for Mark to leave Tania like that, and I thought about the movie, *The Godfather*, in which a son goes to Sicily and meets the girl he subsequently marries, explaining it by saying he was touched by lightning. Well, I looked at it in the same way, and figured my son must have felt something like that. But the news that I was going to be the grandmother of twins was wonderful. And I thought about how strange it was that one of my daughters had four boys, my other daughter's only child was a boy, and now my son was going to have twin boys. I completely joined in his happiness.

It was September of 1995 when Mark called, telling me he was back in California. Eva had gotten back before he did and was already out of the navy. They were going to be married in Santa Barbara where her family lived and we were invited to their wedding in October. I sent out only a few invitations: it was going to be a small wedding because neither of them could afford a big one.

So Jacki, Michele and I flew out to California, where we met my sister-in-law—Allan's brother's wife—who was now widowed as well. My very best friend, Josie, and her husband, Bob, also came. I had met them twenty years earlier when I was living in Florida, and since then, they had moved to Palm Springs and were able to fly up to Santa Barbara for the wedding.

Bill and his girlfriend couldn't make it because they had a commitment to be at another wedding, but Lew served as Mark's best man and another friend who was also a SEAL stood in the ceremony. Bill hadn't been too happy about Mark getting married anyway. He thought it was happening too fast and that Mark didn't know what he was doing. Bill was always protective of him, and Mark felt that was why he didn't attend, but the fact was that he did have to go to the other wedding.

Jacki, Michele and I went to a hotel in Santa Barbara and met Mark and his future wife in the lobby. I remember him coming towards me wearing short shorts and a tee-shirt, not something that I had seen him in before. But it was typical of the SEALs, and he looked good. I hadn't seen him in two years, because he had constantly been assigned to different places.

There was a lot of unrest going on in the world at that time. Most of the time I didn't know where my son was, so it was quite a thrill to see him again. I grabbed him and kissed him. Then he introduced the three of us to Eva. She looked lovely, and it was hardly apparent that she was pregnant.

I put my hand on her tummy and said that it was so good to finally meet her, adding that she should let me know if there was anything I could do for her. I couldn't tell whether she liked me or not, but we had a pleasant enough conversation, mostly about the wedding. Her mother and aunt were there to help her and they were going to have the ceremony at a church, followed by a reception in the backyard of her aunt's house.

I had bought Eva a gold chain that had a charm on it with the faces of two little boys. I wanted to give it to her that day, but Michele cautioned me not to do that right away because you never know when expecting twins. She suggested that I wait until they were born, but I dismissed the thought, said nothing bad would happen, and went ahead and gave it to her. (Since then, incidentally, I have learned to heed Michele's instincts because she's often right.)

The night before the wedding, Michele invited the entire wedding party to a wonderful French restaurant in downtown Santa Barbara. I was glad she did, because I don't think I could have afforded it at the time, but Michele and Jacki always looked out for their brother. Jacki had heard that they didn't have any music lined up for the reception, so she hired a girl who played guitar. The dinner was splendid. We had a long, cozy table of family and friends and everybody got up and gave a speech. Mark felt bad that Bill wasn't there, but he was glad that Lew and his other SEAL friend came.

The next morning we got up early and got ready for the wedding. All of us had to squeeze into one car. The outdoor ceremony was beautiful and everything went well. The only thing that was disappointing was that the pastor Mark knew was sick and he wasn't familiar with the woman who filled in for him.

Then we left the church and headed for the reception. It was a wonderful day. The back yard of Eva's aunt's house was beautifully decorated. Shortly after everything was underway, the guitarist arrived and the entertainment started. Mark played and sang a few songs, too. Then they asked me to sing a French song, so I sang an old favorite, *La Vie en Rose.*

Everyone had a good time, and later in the day we went into the house to watch Mark and Eva open their gifts. Two days later, I went home to enjoy my grandchildren. It didn't matter how far away my kids were, as long as they were happy. So Jacki went back to Florida and Michele and I went back to Petoskey.

When I got home, I called the insurance company and told them that Mark had just turned thirty-five and had $15,000 coming from a policy of his dad's. I was glad that the money was coming at such an appropriate time, just when he had married and was starting a new life.

At first, the insurance company wasn't quick to respond. Mark was only seven years old when his father died and the policy had been drafted five years before that. So I ended up having to call my nephew who worked for the company. He then called our local office and told them they owed Mark the money and they needed to make good on it. And they finally did.

Everything was going according to plan. Mark and Eva moved into the upstairs apartment of a building owned by another SEAL. It was fairly small, but they decided to take it until they could find something bigger because it was close to the base and within walking distance of the ocean. Mark still loved to surf, so the location near the ocean was ideal.

Because the apartment was small, though, Mark had to do something with his piano. He gave it to a coffee house with the stipulation that he play it there whenever he wanted. In order to get the piano to the restaurant, he had to put it on his skateboard and roll it down the middle of the street for about half a mile. But he made it, and every weekend he'd go there to relax and play his piano.

One evening, about two weeks after he was married, Mark called me from Balboa Naval Hospital. He sounded frantic. He had taken Eva there because she was having contractions. They kept her for a little while, but said that it was false labor and wanted to discharge her. Mark didn't know what he should do. I coaxed him to try to get them to keep her for the night, and told him she should relax as much as possible.

He told the doctor what I said, but she refused, saying that he had to take her home because she was fine. Since the doctor was an officer, she pulled rank on Mark and they had to leave against his better judgment.

He called me when they got home, and Eva was still not doing well. Then, at around five in the morning, he called me again, sounding more frantic, and said that Eva's pains had gotten worse and that he'd taken her back to the hospital. There was no doubt this time that she was in labor.

I was devastated by the sound of his voice and felt terrible for both of them. I also asked if there was anything the doctors could do to stop the premature labor, but Mark told me there wasn't. I could tell he was furious that they hadn't kept her at the hospital in the first place. He told me he'd had to carry her up the stairs to the apartment after their initial trip and that, shortly afterward, her contractions had begun again and were worse than before.

About three hours after Mark took her back to the hospital, Eva gave birth to two infant boys. They were only five-and-a-half months along and couldn't survive. I was even sadder when Mark told me how he thought his twins were going to replace the loss of his dad, and how happy he would have been. Eva was feeling terrible, as well, and Mark stayed with her, sleeping beside her in the hospital bed.

We were all surprised that the doctor had sent Eva home. Michele said she'd never heard of any hospital doing that to anyone who was expecting twins, especially when they were in any kind of danger. I explained to her that Mark had tried everything he could and that, because the doctor was an officer, Mark's hands had been tied.

The next morning, I talked to Mark again. He told me he had run into the doctor and she had said, "Well, I guess I made a bad call." Mark told me that he had stared at her and said, "Yes, you really made a bad call." After that, they decided that no matter what happened, no one in their family would ever go to Balboa Hospital again.

When Eva was able to go back to their apartment, her mother stayed with her until she could get back on her feet. According to Eva, she and her mother had never gotten along, so she didn't stay any longer than necessary. Still, Mark appreciated her being there. It seemed that her mother was a caring woman who had come running when her daughter was in trouble. All that was certain was that Mark and Eva's loss was very hard on both of them.

Three months passed and Mark was about to be deployed again. When I talked to him, he said it was probably a good thing he was leaving, because since both he and Eva were so depressed, they weren't helping each other. He said he'd been told that when children are lost it takes a toll on the marriage, and he understood what they were talking about. But he was determined to try his best.

Then two weeks before he was scheduled to leave, I called to say I was thinking about going to California. I figured I could take them out to eat a few times and perhaps be of some comfort. So I asked Mark if it would be okay for me to visit and he said that it was, but I wanted to make sure it would be alright with Eva as well. Even though he assured me that it would, I asked him to let me talk to her and she said it was fine. Then I talked to Michele, who wasn't sure it was a good idea. I told her that Eva had said it was fine, but Michele wasn't convinced, and thought that I should ask again, just to make certain that I'd be welcome. So I called back. This time I talked to Mark again and once more he assured me that everything would be fine. In fact, he sounded real happy that I'd be coming. So my mind was made up. It would be good to see my boy again. Except for the three days of his wedding, I hadn't seen him much in two years. Now he was about to leave for six months and I could tell that he was in a lot of anguish.

I arrived at the San Diego airport around noon to discover that no one was on hand to welcome me. I was beginning to wonder if I had given Mark the right time, when I saw him coming toward me with two other young men. We hugged, and he introduced me to his friends. Then he explained that he hadn't renewed the insurance on his truck, since he would be leaving in three weeks and would be gone for six months. He said that Eva had taken the car to school and that his friend, who also had a truck, would take us back to the apartment.

I took them to lunch at one of the airport's restaurants and then we headed out. It turned out that the truck didn't have a back seat, so I sat in the back of the cab on a board that served as a makeshift seat. It would've been alright, but it seemed that Mark's friend was determined to hit every bump and pothole along the way. At one point, he struck such a big one that I was bounced off the seat, and when I came down, I hurt my side so badly that I thought I'd broken a rib.

Mark's friends dropped us off at the apartment and the two of us went upstairs. Almost immediately I sensed that something wasn't right with him. I told Mark, and he said that Eva had been nervous about my coming. I asked him why he hadn't told me before, and said I wouldn't have come if it was going to cause a problem. But he said it was okay: Eva was just under a lot of pressure with her classes and the loss of the babies.

The apartment was small, beautiful, and very clean. It was also very organized, which was something I had ever known Mark to be. I assumed it was in pristine condition for my arrival, and told Mark with a chuckle, "You know, I didn't come here with a white glove to do an inspection. I came to get to know Eva better and get closer to her, and to see you before you leave. After all, I'll be here five days and that's it."

He assured me again that everything would be fine, but the look on his face betrayed his words and I became concerned that Eva really didn't want me around. Still, I thought I could convince her that I had just come to be helpful. I had always gotten along with Mark's girlfriends, because if he loved someone, I loved them, too. In fact, I still felt close Patty, who would call me from time to time. So I really believed that things would be okay with Eva and me. I loved everybody and I thought everybody would love me. I guess that was my mistake.

Mark showed me around the apartment. He took me down to his beloved ocean. It was less then a block away and the area was beautiful. Then we went to the coffee house where he showed me his piano, and then we went back to the apartment.

Five o'clock came and Eva wasn't home. Six o'clock came and so did seven, and she still didn't arrive. Mark said that her classes had been over at around one, so with each passing hour I felt more and more like an intruder. The two of us were talking in the living room when she finally came home and I got up to give her a hug. When I did, she just gave me a cold, penetrating stare. Until that point, all I had ever seen in her blue eyes was happiness, but the look she gave me there made them seem black. They were so piercing that I will never forget that moment.

I took a step back and thought, *oh boy, this is going to be a mistake. Here it is again, Michele warned me and I didn't listen. I'm an idiot.* So I tried with all my might to be loving. I tried to talk to her. She answered me politely, but with as few words as possible, and I could tell she wasn't at all happy to see me. I told her that I wanted to take them out to eat and she quickly said, "No no, I'm going to make dinner. I already have something planned." I asked her if there was anything I could do, and she snapped, "No, you can't do anything." I became aware of a cold feeling at the base of my spine.

She made a nice dinner, and as we ate, things seemed pleasant again for awhile. I tried hard not to seem intrusive and told them that I wanted to make myself as small as possible. The evening came to a close and they went to bed and I went to sleep on the futon in the living room.

I woke up early the next morning and went for a walk on the pier so I wouldn't be in the way as they got ready for their day. We had our plans where I would take them out to dinner and I was hoping to take them to a nice place where we could relax and things wouldn't be so bad. I had entertained thoughts of staying at a hotel, thinking that it might ease the tension, but I really couldn't afford to do that, and upon further thought I didn't want to make matters worse by making Mark think I was leaving because of Eva. So I didn't know what do and I was walking on eggshells.

That evening came and we went to a very nice place and they seemed to have a good time. Eva was more relaxed and charming and again I felt better about the situation. I reiterated to her that my visit was strictly because Mark was about to leave and that I wanted to get to know her better. When we went back to the apartment I thought that I had won her over; however, after we had all gone to bed, Mark came into the living room and told me that Eva was crying. I was surprised and asked Mark if it was because I was there. He said it wasn't, but I could sense that he was stuck between myself and her and he didn't know what to do. I felt as though I was putting him in a very difficult position. I went to talk to her and said, "Please don't cry. I'm so sorry if I'm intruding and if you want me to leave I will leave," but she insisted that it had nothing to do with me and that she still cried at night because of the loss of their babies.

The next morning was Saturday—St. Patrick's Day. We decided to go to the mall and started to browse around. We passed a beauty salon and I offered to buy Eva something for her hair but she refused. We went past another store that had a chair that caught Mark's eye. He sat in it and began a whimsical banter with the saleslady, and they were laughing and I was laughing, but Eva was not amused at all. She walked out of the store and said, "Mark is such an extrovert," and I said, "Yes, he is," but I felt like she didn't like his sense of humor—nor mine. I said that she was probably the opposite and reminded her that opposites attract. After that she didn't talk to me at all and she went to Mark and said that I had insulted her, and that was the last thing in the world that I wanted to do.

When we got back to the apartment Mark asked if I'd like to see him jump. I had never seen him skydive and I wasn't sure if it was a good thing for me to see, but I knew it was important to him so I said yes. At that point Eva got very angry and said, "What do you mean, you're going to take your mother to see you jump?" Mark asked her to come along too and she said, "No, I'm not going to go with you," and to my discomfort, they had a fight in front of me. She walked out of the apartment, got in her car and left. I felt absolutely awful but Mark said, "It's okay, Mom. We'll spend St. Patrick's Day together."

It had been a long time since I'd felt so bad. I asked Mark what was going on and asked if it was still from the loss of the twins and he said, "No, she had a bad temper before and she's seldom in a good mood." I could see that their relationship wasn't all that good, even though I'm sure they loved each other. I told him that I'd made a mistake in coming to San Diego. I told him that I was going to go back to Michigan and said he should go after his wife. He decided to wait a few hours and he took me to a bar and I met some of his SEAL friends. Then we went to Brown's Field and I got to see him skydive. It was an amazing thing for me to see, as well as horrifying—my son jumping out of an airplane. We went back to the apartment, and when Eva wasn't home, Mark called her mother and, sure enough, she was there. I said to Mark, "I'm going to leave now, so you go to her."

Then I called my friend Josie in Palm Springs and told her what was happening. She said she would come get me in her husband's plane. My heart was broken, but both my daughters told me that sometimes it goes that way with daughters-in-law. I didn't understand it because I got along so well with my son-in-law, and I thought we could all be friends as well as family. I didn't know what to do, but Jacki and Michele told me not to do anything. They said it might work itself out in due time.

I told Josie that this was the most difficult situation I'd been through in a long time, and explained that I didn't know how I should act and that Eva didn't like me at all. She laughed when I told her I had thought everyone liked me, and that the one person I wanted to impress favorably had apparently ended up despising me. I was so upset that I was going to go straight home, but Josie talked me into going back to Palm Springs with her. (And so I did, and I spent a relaxing two days with her and her husband before flying home.)

When I returned to Petoskey, Mark told me that Eva had rejoined him at the apartment and the two of them seemed to be doing okay. Then, one day after he left on his six-month deployment, I called Eva to see how she was doing. She was so cold to me over the phone that I finally said to her, "Listen, if you don't like me, I won't call you anymore. Just tell me." She didn't say anything so I said, "Okay then, goodbye," and I hung up.

A while later, I heard from Mark, who was back in Guam. He told me that Eva had flown out there to surprise him. That made me feel better, though she hadn't called to tell me she was going. Nor did she call me when she returned to let me know how Mark was doing. She simply wanted nothing to do with me.

I waited another six months until Mark returned from his tour of duty, and then I wrote her a letter saying that since we both loved Mark, it would be nice if we could get along. I told her that I was sorry if I had done anything to offend her, and that I really wished she would talk to me.

Since she didn't reply, I wrote her another letter—with the same result. Finally, my daughters said to me, "Mom, just let it go. Your son loves you and he always will, and if she doesn't, there's nothing you can do." So, reluctantly, I heeded their advice.

One day, Mark called to say that he was coming home for a week to do some skiing. I asked if he was bringing Eva, but he said she didn't want to come. So I told him that was alright and it would be good to see him. He flew in the following week and it was great to have him back in Michigan. He skied and had a good time. And every day he called Eva.

One night when we were at Michele's for dinner, he called Eva and she was crying because he was away. We told him to tell her we'd pay for her ticket if she wanted to come and spend the last two days of the week with him. Although she declined this offer, Mark had told us when we had met him at the airport she said she would come the next time he visited. Being the optimist that I am, I thought of that as a breakthrough and figured that once she came here, she would see that we all liked her. So it was with joy that I learned Mark was coming back the following Christmas, and that Eva would be coming with him. I was so surprised and happy I could hardly stand it. They did come, and Jacki came up from Florida, too. To my delight, Eva indeed loved Petoskey. She loved the old-fashioned Christmas atmosphere as she went shopping with Mark in the gaslight district downtown. The town was lit up in a festive celebration, there was snow on the ground, the houses in the neighborhood were decked out, and in the end, Eva said it was the best Christmas she'd had in a long time. She was absolutely charming and all I ever saw during that visit was a smile on her face. I thought that perhaps it had taken her a year to understand that Mark wasn't about to leave his family and that she might as well be friendly with us.

When they got back to California, Mark found out that he was about to be deployed again, this time to Malaysia. And when he returned from that assignment, he joined the navy's elite skydiving team, The Leap Frogs. I had always worried about his being a SEAL because, although I hardly ever even knew where he was, I did know that he was doing dangerous things. However, his being in the Leap Frogs was a source of even greater concern for me, because they sometimes did nine or ten practice jumps a day before they even got to their scheduled event, and I always thought that the more you did something like that, the more likely you were to have an accident. "Mom," Mark said, trying to reassure me, "we're so well trained that you have no need to worry. I'm so good at what I do that I could land on a Dixie cup. Besides that, I'd never do anything that would jeopardize my safety."

About six months after her joined the Leap Frogs, Mark and his team were going to do a jump into Soldier Field in Chicago. So all of us from Petoskey—Michele, Dan, the four boys and I—went to see him. We checked into one of the downtown hotels and waited for him. When he got there, he looked wonderful.

He and I went out to lunch, and while we were eating he poured his heart out to me. "You know, Mom," he said, "my life as a married man is really not very good. There are too many ups and downs in the relationship. Eva is not well."

I asked if it was because of the twins, the babies they had lost almost two years ago, but he told me that her mood swings had always been incredible, and that when he went surfing, he had to hide the fact or face her wrath. Many times, he said, she had even thrown his friends out of the apartment. And I knew that that was true enough, because Bill had once told me that she had asked him and another friend to leave because they were making too much noise while she was studying in the other room. He added that he didn't think Eva liked him. And I had told him not to worry, that she was having a hard time after the loss of the twins. But I also felt that her loss was becoming an excuse to behave as she pleased.

Then Mark told me that Eva was going into counseling, and that she definitely didn't want to have any more children. That was really hard for him to hear. I tried to calm him down but he said, "She told me that she doesn't want to have any more children because I'm a child myself and I wouldn't be capable of being a good father."

I felt she had landed a low blow when she had said that, but I tried to tell Mark that sometimes things change and work out. But he was adamant as he assured me that he was going to have a child by the time he was forty and that he didn't care if it was with Eva or someone else.

At that, I decided to let it go. I let him talk out his frustrations, but I never said too much. I knew he still loved her and I didn't want to say anything that could interfere because I still hoped that everything would work out. Besides, Mark was of age and competent to handle his own problems.

The next day we all went to see Mark jump, and before he left, Mark showed us the plane he'd be jumping from and introduced us to the team of skydivers. They all looked impressive in their white suits, but of course I thought that Mark was the most handsome. He was constantly training and was in the best physical shape of his life.

We went to the stadium and took our front-row seats. And when we watched them jump from such a long distance, they looked like nothing more than dots in the sky. But as they came closer, we could see their incredible formations. Another SEAL described each maneuver over the P.A. system and announced which Leap Frog was doing each particular move. I anxiously wondered when they would open their parachutes, as it seemed they were precariously close to the ground. When I saw them finally burst open, I was so relieved. It was a spectacular thing to witness, but as a mother, I was keenly aware of the potential danger involved, and I wished that Mark had a different occupation. However, we all knew how much he loved to jump and to be part of the skydiving team. A man has to do what a man has to do.

After witnessing his performance, we headed back to Petoskey. Everyone had had a good time, but I was concerned about my son.

The Leap Frogs' next venue was in Fort Lauderdale. Mark was delighted to go back and see his sister, Jacki, nephew Nicholas, and all his friends. All the boys he had gone to school with came to see him, and the Leap Frogs were shown on the Jumbotron during the Dolphins' game. His friend told me they looked like rock stars, all dressed in white and signing autographs after they had finished.

On Mother's Day of 1997, Mark called me and said his marriage was in even worse condition than before and that he was thinking about getting a divorce. In fact, he was making plans to move out of the apartment and into the jump team's quarters. He said he couldn't take the ups and downs of Eva's moods anymore. When I asked him if their problems could be fixed, he said, "I don't know, but I really don't think so." I tried to tell him that sometimes things get better, but there was no way I could console him. It was clear that he was furious with her. In the end, I let him talk and he got everything off his chest. Then he wished me a happy Mother's Day.

That was the last time I heard from him before his accident.

THE ACCIDENT

It was a Saturday—May seventeenth, 1997—a Saturday not unlike any other. My little dog Maggie and I had been in the backyard all day. I was planting flowers, celebrating the end of a long winter and the arrival of warmer days. At sixty-nine years of age I was enjoying a peaceful life. I tutored French from my home and taught it twice a week at the Montessori school that two of my grandchildren attended.

So on that awful day in May, I didn't have one of those intuitions that a mother is supposed to have. I think it was three or four in the afternoon when Mark's best friend Bill called. I had known Bill since he was ten years old and he and Mark together had always been mischievous. As a consequence, I thought at first that he was kidding when he told me that Mark had been in an accident. But when I asked if he was kidding and I heard the tone of his voice, my legs started to get weak. He told me that it had happened during a jump and that Mark's hand was in awful shape, but he thought he was going to make it. Terrible thoughts went through my mind, but then I thought, *His hand? Okay, but what about his life?*

It seems that Mark had been doing training jumps at Brown Field with two other SEALs. One of them, a relatively inexperienced Leap Frog, had jumped after Mark and was free falling in Mark's airspace when Mark opened his parachute, which is like putting on the brakes. The SEAL above came crashing into him, tore through his parachute and hit him in the head and hand with his legs.

There was urgency in Bill's voice, like he wanted me to be there. I was struggling to keep from falling to pieces as I was trying to take in everything that he told me, and I said, "Let me talk to his wife." I asked her what she thought and she said that they wouldn't let anyone see him until they had evaluated his condition. She was probably in shock, because she said, "Oh, he's going to be sore."

When I heard that, I thought, *well, he's going to be sore, but at least he's alright.* Then I asked her to let me talk with Bill again and I told him I was calling the airlines, and that Michele and I would be there as soon as possible. Despite the information I tried to get out of Bill and Eva, I still didn't know what to think.

I phoned Michele, but she was out of town at a soccer tournament with her husband and kids and it took two hours before I was able to reach her. Meanwhile, I called the airlines, but there were no flights to San Diego that night. I also tried every nearby airport but there wasn't anything until seven the next morning. Then I called Jacki in Florida and told her what had happened. She was devastated and said she would meet us in San Diego, but it turned out that she couldn't get a flight until morning either.

I booked two seats for the morning flight, one for Michele and one for me. She was two hours out of town and was coming in as fast as she could. Meanwhile, she had called my neighbor and another friend and asked them to stay with me because she knew how upset I was. But I was already in denial. I really thought Mark was going to be okay. *Maybe it's just his left hand,* I thought, *and he won't be able to play the guitar or piano. That's not so bad.*

Finally, though, I couldn't stand it anymore and called the University Of California San Diego Hospital. I will never forget my conversation with the nurse in charge who said, "You'd better come fast. Your son is very bad. He has several fractures in his back, pelvis and hand, and closed head trauma. Right now we have him stabilized, but we still don't know the total extent of his injuries." When I asked if he would still be alive when I got there the next day, she said, "I won't lie to you, I don't know."

I couldn't bear not being by Mark's side. I called the airlines again and did everything I could think of to arrange a flight, but nothing was available, so the only thing I could do was wait until the morning. I recalled how Mark's father and my sister had died when I wasn't there, and how my mother had died just after I left her. Now I was afraid that my son, too, would die before I could get there and I felt helpless and petrified. My only comfort was that he'd been brought to UCSD, not to Balboa Hospital.

Michele came to get me as soon as she got back into town and I spent that night at her house. She, too, was devastated. We called Jacki and found that she was due to arrive in San Diego at about the same time as we were.

I believe that night at Michele's was the worst night of my life. I felt so helpless. I was twenty-five hundred miles away from my son and there was nothing I could do but pray. I called my niece in France and told her what had happened because I wanted to hear her say that Mark was going to be okay, and of course, that's exactly what she said.

At two in the morning, one of Mark's teammates called me. I could tell he had been drinking and was upset. He asked when I was coming and I told him we wouldn't be able to leave until morning. I felt he was looking to me for comfort.

He told me that Mark always talked about his mom and told me that all the SEALs were in the waiting room of the trauma unit and were praying for him. Hearing him say that made me feel better, because I believe that people who are prayed for have a better chance of recovery. If the SEALs were praying for him, and if I could get everyone at home to pray for him too, there was a chance he'd still be alive when I got there.

Looking out the window as the plane left for San Diego, I wondered how high Mark had been when he fell. I thought again about how Bill had said that his hand was very bad. *So, maybe he'll loose his arm, but he'll be alive!* I thought. I replayed Eva's words, "He's probably going to be sore when he wakes up." *Well, maybe he has a few broken bones. That can be fixed. But what if he never wakes up? No! Please God, I've always asked you not to take my kids before me!*

I couldn't stand it. Micki's face was pale and expressionless and I knew that she was ready for the worst. The same overriding theme was also with her. *God, I will accept him any way he is, but let him be alive.*

Eva picked us up at the airport, and since Jacki was due to arrive only five minutes after we did, we waited for her. Eva was crying and told us they were working on Mark and that she still hadn't been able to see him. She told us what she knew and said they'd told her that Mark wasn't paralyzed. He had been struggling when the paramedics had tried to insert the ventilation tube in his throat, so at least his legs and hands were moving. By the time he arrived at the hospital, however, he had become comatose. They intended to keep him sedated for the first three days, which was a critical period.

It was to Mark's advantage that he was being cared for by a great trauma team at UCSD Hospital, where each specialist was at the top of his or her particular field. And when we got to the waiting room of the trauma unit, there were Navy SEALs everywhere, sitting on the floor, squatting or standing, all waiting and looking at the door that no one could open unless they rang the buzzer. Next to the buzzer was a phone connecting you to a nurse who would tell you if you could enter. Visits were limited to two people at a time for five minutes.

When the door opened, the nurse asked if I was Mark's mom. Then she said, "I want you to be prepared. He's alive, but he's in an induced coma so that he won't feel all the injuries he's sustained. There are a lot of tubes and it might be shocking to see your son like that, but we're trying to save his life."

As she was talking, all I could think was, *He's alive! He's still alive! I just want to go and see him.* I went through the terrifying doors and past four or five rooms where trauma nurses were tending to different patients, following the nurse who took me all the way around the corridor to where my son was. It was a shock to see him. He had nothing on except a pillowcase over his groin. His face was very swollen, which made him look—for a split second—a little bit like his dad had when he was in his coffin. Suddenly I realized that Allan had died at the same age as Mark was now, and for a fleeting moment it was like a knife in my heart. But then I touched Mark's right hand and it was warm, so my hope returned.

His strong, beautiful body didn't have a mark on it. His hair was shaved halfway to the middle of his head, to which tubes were attached. His left hand was bandaged up to his elbow, so I couldn't see the damage to it. He was wearing a halo. I didn't know what a halo was then, but it looked horrible and painful. It was screwed into his head and connected to a vest-like device by metal bars. It almost looked like the vest of a Viking with the fur on the inside.

Moe, the nurse who was taking care of Mark, said, "You can talk to him. He might hear you from afar and sense your presence,"

"Mark darling, we're all here," I said as I stood at the side of his bed. "We love you. Mom's here and you're going to be okay. Mark, hang on! You're strong!"

The five minutes were over so fast. I had very little time to ask more questions but I knew that it was serious. No one there could tell me what was going to happen; the nurse said I would have to talk to the doctor. When I got back to the hall outside of the trauma room, I saw Bill, and he looked very worried. We hugged each other and then every SEAL gave me a hug, and then they hugged Michele and Jacki as well. They began to tell me stories about Mark, and said that if anybody would make it, he would, because he was such an incredible guy. They were a tremendous comfort to me. It was as if Mark was speaking through them saying, "Mom, I'll be okay. Listen to my guys. They know.

A team of doctors came out of intensive care and asked to talk to his family. What they told us was frightening. Mark had a broken neck, a broken pelvis, two broken vertebrae in the middle of his back, a bruised lung and—most significant of all—a severe brain injury, the extent of which they wouldn't know until he came out of the induced coma. His left arm was broken and his fingers were so damaged that they would have to operate to put them back together. But he was not paralyzed.

They had ordered a special bed for him, one that continuously moved back and forth from right to left to keep his circulation going. They told us that the next three days were going to be critical because the brain usually swells from trauma.

At that moment, I think I experienced the same thing that happened to me when Allan died, because I became two people, the one watching myself from afar who didn't feel it was real, and the one who went through all the horror and pain. It was a pain I knew all too well from the loss of my husband, my sister and mother. But the thought of losing one of my children was the most terrible pain I could imagine. Michele had had a life threatening skiing accident a few years earlier, but at least I had been able to talk to her the next day, and I realized that it was nothing compared to what Mark was up against.

The next three days were a nightmare as we waited to see if Mark's brain would swell. He was in a special bed, and a panel had been placed under each of his armpits to keep his body from falling to one side or the other. I had a chance to look at his halo more closely and see the screws that went into his head. That sight was more than this mother could bear. His leg was suspended in the air and long metal screws had been inserted on both sides of his knee. On each side, there were weights pulling on his hip. His left arm was in a cast and only the tips of his fingers were showing.

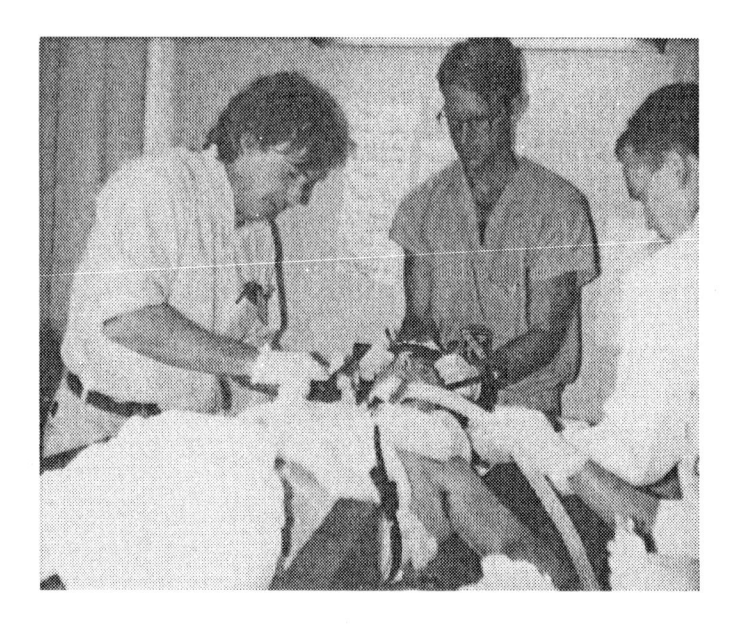

Every hour, two people at a time could go in and see him, except between twelve and two in the afternoon when no one could go in. Then the visits began again and continued until about six or seven p.m. I can't remember exactly because time was of no consequence to me. All I know is the wait each time before I saw him was difficult. Sometimes I'd let other people go in my place because it made me feel good to have his friends see him. Sometimes I went in with Eva, other times with Jacki or Michele, and sometimes with Bill. Still other times, I went in with one of the SEALs.

Mark seemed to have two or three nurses around him at all times, and they constantly monitored his blood pressure. Moe told me that it had been alternating between high and low, that it depended on how much pain Mark was in, and they would give him morphine whenever it got too high. It was hard to imagine someone in a coma feeling any pain and it was hard to accept that it was happening to Mark. He had tubes everywhere, but his color was good. He wasn't moving at all, and his arms were at his sides. I would take his hand in mine and squeeze it. It was warm and it felt good to hold.

Eva was devastated. Clearly, she didn't know that Mark had confided in me about their marital problems and I felt terrible because I could tell she was very upset. I knew that things didn't always go smoothly in a marriage and I also knew that Mark was no angel. I also realized that it was difficult to be married to someone who was deployed for six months at a time, so having her beside me and seeing her concern, I let go of everything Mark had told me. When two of the SEALs told me they knew of Mark's plans to get a divorce and asked what was going to happen with it, I told them that nothing was going to happen for the moment. All I was concerned about was that Mark got well. Then he could take care of the matter on his own. They knew to leave it at that.

The first day, Eva was very obliging. At the end of the evening she took us to an apartment that belonged to friends who were moving into a new apartment. We could use it for two nights, but we had to make other arrangements after that. Michele, Jacki and I stayed there that night, but none of us slept well. Michele said we'd have to make plans for me to stay near the hospital, and that she would be able to stay a couple of weeks, then could come back again after she went home for a while. We didn't know the extent of Mark's brain injury but it didn't sound like I'd be going home any time soon.

It was good to have Michele around. She could talk to the doctors and nurses and understand all the terminology. Without her, I would have been completely in the dark. I hadn't known anyone who'd had a brain injury and I didn't know any of the signs to watch for or their ramifications. All I knew was that my son was in an induced coma and that he could come out of it in three days. The only reassuring thing was that he still looked so strong, even with his eyes closed. When Mark and Eva had come to Petoskey six months earlier, I noticed that he was in the best shape of his life—190 pounds of pure muscle. And lying there in the hospital, he was the same handsome man we were used to seeing. It almost seemed like nothing had happened to him. He had no cuts besides those on his left arm and hand, and they were in a cast so we couldn't see them. I thanked God for that, because I don't think I could have handled seeing my boy's hand so badly mangled.

Bill was a great source of comfort to all of us. As soon as he heard what had happened, he called the airlines and canceled his flights. By that time, he was a commercial pilot, and he told the airline he was going to stay with his brother, which was almost the truth because he had always told everyone that Mark was his brother, and he certainly acted like one. The next day he picked us up at the apartment and took us to the hospital. All of Mark's Navy SEAL friends were already there when we arrived and it was so uplifting for us to see that so many people cared. Bill said that his fiancée, whom I had never met, was going to come to the hospital sometime during the day.

As word of the accident got out, some of Mark's non-SEAL friends began to appear and the waiting room was constantly filled with friends and teammates. Eva's mother had been there the day before we arrived, but by the time we got there, she was gone. I heard that Eva had told her she wasn't needed anymore.

Eva acted like everything had been okay between Mark and her before the accident, and there was no hint that she harbored any animosity toward me or the rest of his family. Mark, however, had told me that she had two personalities. In fact, I recall seeing her self-portrait. She had painted an extremely harsh look on her face. Mark had told me how accurately it depicted the one side of her and that the other Eva was very nice. "But when that one emerges, watch out," he had warned.

So far, however, we had only experienced the good and sweet Eva and she looked genuinely worried. That was all I needed to see—that she loved Mark and was kind to him.

On the second day, Eva told me I could stay with her after Michele and Jacki left. But I didn't think about it too much because their apartment was a long way from the hospital and I wanted to be closer. I also didn't want to think about where to stay until the next day, when Mark was supposed to come out of his coma.

That afternoon, Mark's officers from the SEALs, along with another officer from the navy, came to the hospital in their uniforms. They were very nice, but the sight of them in their formal attire aroused fear in me because it seemed to confirm what a dangerous condition Mark was in. They assured me that they would do anything in their power to assist me, and said we could stay for a week at the officer's hotel on the base and that they'd have someone take us back and forth between the hotel and the hospital whenever we needed. I thanked them and said that perhaps I'd move there with Michele after Jacki went back to Florida. Still, it was hard to think about anything like that. In fact, it was difficult for me to function at all. I never seemed to know where I was or what was going on. All I could ever think was, *Please, Mark, wake up from your coma.*

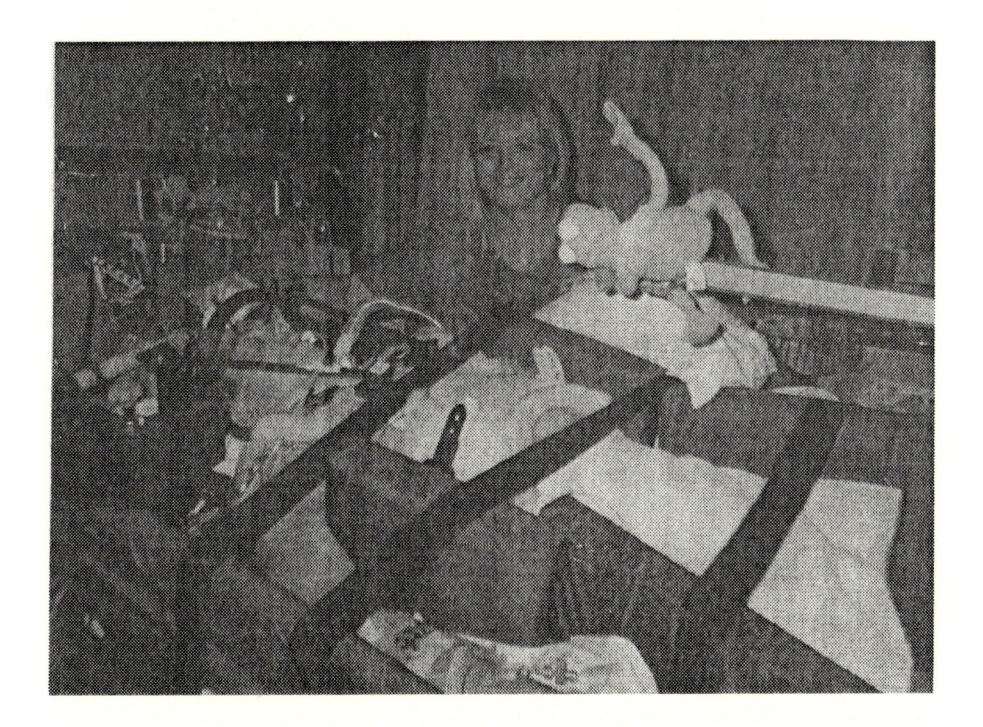

From the time she got on the plane to San Diego, Jacki began keeping a journal, and wrote her first entry the day after the accident:

My dearest brother Mark,

Today is Sunday, May 18th and I'm sitting on a plane to Houston where I will connect to San Diego to see you after your horrible accident yesterday. I'm writing this because I know you are in a coma right now fighting for your life and I <u>pray</u> that you will be able to read this and it's helping me cope.

I can't bear the thought of losing you, my precious brother. The sun shines when you are around. Micki and Mom are flying on another plane from Detroit.

Mom is a basket case and says if you go she will go next to you. You know you are her favorite—<u>all</u> of <u>our</u> <u>favorites</u>. Bill Devitt will pick us up and you will have all of the people who love you at your bedside helping you to fight this horrible accident.

I keep thinking of the air show when I surprised you at the hotel and then how great you looked in your white suit. You were giving Fred the high-five and you looked like you were having a blast and you kept asking me if I was hot because I was wearing black. I was so proud of you and happy to see you.

And I'm so happy you came over the time before and stayed at my house. I love you so much. I used to stroll you around when you were a baby.

Mark you have to make it! You have to make it! I'm so sad for your broken neck and bones. I don't know what went wrong. I want to see the video to see what moron jumped on you. This flight is an <u>eternity</u>—I can't wait to be near you with Mom and Micki. You won't know it but we'll be by your side pulling for you. It took us twenty years to lose the pain of losing your dad and now this—I can't go through it again. You've got to pull through. Fight please, Mark! Fight with all you've got!

You need to have kids yet so you can have someone driving you nuts like mine. I'm finally leaving for San Diego. I'm afraid to see you and the terrible shape you are in. They put you in a coma so you can heal and so you don't move. You are in God's hands now. We can only pray and be with you. We love you so much.

I know you will read this someday because you are <u>tough.</u> I bought you an angel in Texas to give you more luck. Time is everything. I think about what a good brother you have been, trying to help me with my problems with Nick. Calling the doctor for me and sitting down with him and trying to give him advice about how to act in life. Nicholas is very upset too and wanted to come, but I know that it wouldn't be good for either one of you. I know your life is going to be very hard for a long time and now I want to help you—no matter what.

I remember when you sang **Moondance**. I love when you sing and I love that you are so talented. Maybe you think this is silly—my writing this—but I want you to know what was happening while you were asleep. And I want you to know how much I adore you, my special brother and I can't stand the thought that you might pass away before we get there—I couldn't bear it. You have to make it!

Later that afternoon, a good looking young man on crutches and favoring his right leg came into the waiting room. He was in tears, and one of the SEALs told me he was the person who had crashed into Mark. I could see that his knee was black and blue, and as I looked at it, I realized it was the knee that had hit Mark in the head. He was very sorry and I felt bad for him. It's always sad to see a man crying the way he was, so we hugged each other. He said he had passed out, but had come to after going through Mark's parachute and had been able to land okay. As a result, he had no broken bones—just some bruising to his knee—nothing compared to Mark's injuries. He only stayed a few minutes because he was so upset, and then left with another SEAL.

Michele was my rock. She was always calm, even though she was just as upset as I was. She'd explain to me what was happening, keeping me up to date on Mark's condition, and was always full of hope. "You'll see," she kept saying, "Mark's going to be okay. He's going to get well. He's strong and he'll surprise everyone and come out of this. I refuse to give up on him." It made me feel good to hear her say that. She gave me confidence and encouragement at a time when I needed it most.

She was also making plans for me to stay there for the long haul. Her husband was kind enough to take care of their four boys by himself during the two weeks she was in San Diego, but she couldn't extend her stay beyond that. Jacki, too, had to get back to her teaching job.

When the third day came, we knew a lot of things were going to happen. We'd know if fluid was accumulating in Mark's brain, and we'd find out if he would come out of the induced coma as scheduled. When we arrived at the hospital that morning, we were very anxious. It was still very early, but we wanted to go in to see him as soon as we were permitted. Eva met us there, and we went inside the ICU together and asked to speak with the doctor.

"Well, the good news is that Mark didn't have any accumulation of fluid or swelling on his brain, which is very unusual with an injury like this," he said. "That's a good sign because it would have made his brain injury worse."

I was so glad to hear it, but the doctor had more to tell us.

"The bad news is that he hasn't come out of the coma yet and he should have about an hour ago. But it's still possible that he will, so we're not going to feel too bad about it yet."

We left the meeting unsure of what to think.

Again, two at a time, we went in to see Mark. When we got to the room, Moe said that they were trying to wake him up. She was pressing a pencil against his fingernails, and as she did, she said, "Talk to him real loud and try to wake him up." I bent down to him and said, "Mark, Mark! Please wake up Mark! Come on Mark, come out of this…please wake up!" But we didn't get any response. He looked like he was sleeping deeply, and only the bed was moving. The noise from all the machines and equipment was horrible, especially the suction for his tracheotomy machine. If anyone has ever had someone they loved with a trach., they will understand how difficult it is to witness this suctioning process. There were always bells and different monitor alarms going off, and it seemed like every time I had five minutes with him, some alarm would ring and I would think, *Oh my God, this is the end.*

Moe was with Mark all the time. She had a terrific personality and she knew what she was doing. So the five minutes were always spent staring at him, holding his hand and pleading, "Please Mark, wake up."

During the two-hour period in the afternoon when no one could go into the room, Michele, Jacki and I would go to lunch, and Eva would go back to her apartment to feed her parrot. Our lunches were never very relaxing, though, because each of us was agonizing over what was happening and what could happen to Mark. Sometimes we'd go downstairs to the cafeteria and other times we'd just walk. Michele was a runner and she thought a little exercise would be good for me, so we'd walk for about a mile, stop and grab a bite at a restaurant and then walk back. Regardless of where we went, my head was always back at the hospital thinking, *Maybe he's going to wake up today.*

On this third day, when we got back, I was surprised to see that all the SEALs were gone. I asked Bill, "What happened? Isn't anyone staying to see Mark today?" And he said, "Eva had one of her fits and told everyone to leave. I guess the old Eva has finally surfaced."

I was surprised, but I wanted to give her the benefit of the doubt. I figured that she was a private person and was bothered by the fact that the SEALs were taking up so much of the visitation time. I missed having them there, however, because they were such a source of comfort for me, but I also knew that Eva didn't like having other people around. It made her crazy. One time, when she came out from her five-minute visit, she said to me in a very strange voice, "I know that I said that you could stay at our apartment, but I don't think it's a good idea." I was caught off guard by it and thought, *Oh boy, I must have said or did something and here we go again. She hates me.* I was too involved in my son's situation to worry about Eva and her ups and downs. I knew we were all upset about Mark and I thought that it might be her way of dealing with his situation: I needed people; she didn't like them.

That afternoon, a beautiful young woman with long, black hair came up to me in the waiting room and said, "I'm Sandy, Bill's fiancée." She put her arms around me and I immediately felt warmth from her. I knew right away that I was going to like her and that Bill had made a very good choice. She was as sweet as she was lovely. Unfortunately, when Eva spotted her, she got the same strange look on her face that she had in her self-portrait, and I sensed that something was going on between the two of them. Later, Bill told me that his upcoming wedding had been an issue between Eva and Mark. He wanted to go to Bill's wedding, which was going to be in Hawaii, but Eva didn't want to because Bill had not gone to theirs. Mark had told Bill not to worry, that he'd be there with or without Eva.

Just like Mark, Bill had many friends. I remember one in particular, who was nick-named Foot. He was a handsome young commercial pilot about six-foot one, who was as nice as can be. He came to the hospital with Bill many times, bringing presents for Mark and comfort to us. He told us how he used to bike and surf with Mark and that they had become very good friends. I wasn't surprised, every one of Bill's friends was a friend of Mark's, and vice versa.

That afternoon when it was time for Eva and I to go into Mark's room, she came to me and said, "I want to be alone with my husband." I could see that her patience was running thin; we were just so different. I never minded having someone else go in with me. I thought the more people in the room, the better the chance that Mark would wake up. The more love he got, the better off he would be.

The navy chaplain came to see Mark and prayed with us. He said that Mark's story had been on the news the night before and he told us about their account: *Two Navy SEALs collided in a skydiving accident and were taken by ambulance to the hospital where one was released and one remains in critical condition.* At that time, though, I didn't want to see the news clip that the paramedics had filmed during Mark's rescue.

Mark had been on his last jump of the day when the accident happened. They were about to go home, but then the three of them decided to make one more jump. One of the SEALs who had come to see Mark told me that he had seen the whole thing. He felt as though he was paralyzed, because he had already opened his chute, and that rendered him unable to help. If he had been skydiving, he could have reached Mark because they had learned how to do that in their training, but he was helpless once his chute was open. He told me that only two of the ten cells in Mark's parachute had remained functional, and that he had twirled down three-thousand feet at eighty to ninety miles an hour. He also told me how, when he got to the ground, he had had to dig dirt out of Mark's mouth so that he could breathe.

Photo taken months before Mark's accident

Someone had called the ambulance, which arrived quickly. They tried to get a tube in Mark's mouth, but he fought them. When I heard that, I hoped that the fight he had in him would help him through his ordeal and bring him out of the coma.

After hearing this first-hand account, I called the ambulance company and asked them to thank the paramedics who had tended to Mark. They told me that no one had ever called to thank them before, and that they would tell the ones who had been on the scene. Later that afternoon, the two paramedics came to the hospital and asked the nurse how Mark was doing. I wasn't there at the time, but I was very grateful to them for it.

The fourth day came and all I could do was squeeze Mark's hand. For a time, I thought I was getting a reaction from him because there'd be a slight hint of a squeeze in return, but the doctor told me that it was just a reflex and not an indication that he was coming out of his coma. Another time, Jacki was visiting and all of a sudden she started screaming because she thought Mark had opened one eye. She came running out of the room shouting, "He opened his eyes! He opened his eyes!" She was yelling so loudly that all the other nurses in the trauma center came out of their rooms and told her to be quiet. I had to calm her down, and when I went into Mark's room, I found out, to my disappointment, that it *was* simply another reflex and not a sign that he was waking up. I went back into the waiting room and told everyone the news. I saw Eva giving Jacki a look that could kill.

It was obvious that Eva was getting more and more annoyed with us, but I really didn't care. I just wanted to be with my son. Michele was very cordial to her and tried to comfort her. Because of her years as a nurse, she knew how to deal with Eva and her little personality quirks. Plus, Michele has the patience of an angel and tried to keep me on an even keel with Eva. But I was becoming less and less forgiving and it was increasingly apparent that we were not made of the same cloth. I had never known anyone who was so secluded by choice. She didn't have any friends and never wanted anybody to come to her apartment.

When Mark had been well, I could try to ignore Eva's coolness towards me, but on the fourth day after his accident, tired and distraught, her quick change of moods was beginning to get to me, since I realized Mark was going to be in the hospital for a long time and I didn't look forward to being with such a negative person. Usually, I never got involved in my children's relationship problems because I didn't consider it my place. I also figured that, if I did take a side in an argument, the other one would resent me or hold a grudge after the situation was resolved. However, at this point, I felt that Mark was vulnerable and I didn't even know if he was going to make it.

Time passed slowly those first few days. We were all trying so hard to cope with everything that was happening. Jacki decided to ask everyone who visited Mark to write him a little note. These are just a few of the many that were written to him between May 20th and May 25th.

Hey Mark,

Guess who. It's Lew in supply. Thanks, now I have to deal with doing it every day. I've been here for two hours now but you still keep blowing me off. Wait until you see your canopy that landed you, you'll be happy with your injuries. I'm standing here outside and I can see you. Your

family is all waiting for you to wake up. Hurry up and opened your darn eyes.

Lew

Hey Dude,

I've been waiting a couple of hours to see you. Scott King is also here. The nurse allowed us a few minutes to actually visit and I must admit, in all the years we have known each other this is the quietest you've been. I'm in your corner. Take care always.

Your half-brother,

Tom

Mark,

Just wanted to stop by and say hello. Someone else should be by soon. Lots of people have been saying prayers and I hope that you are doing better. Talk to you soon,

Scott King

Hi Mark,

Only a guy tough enough to do the super-frog on the beach cruiser could do what you've done, you wild man. I'll be praying for you. Remember that God is with you and he's spared you for a special purpose—to live for him.

Take care, dude.

Guy Lee "Chaps"

Hey,

I've seen you look worse, buddy. Hope when you read this that you can still remember the long midnight runs and swims out on the beach. See you soon. Tough times don't like tough guys like you. Take care buddy.

Wills

Mark's captain—Captain Yasbrough—was very considerate and spent a lot of time with us. He and his wife came in with a basket of food one day and we ate outside the hospital during a time when we couldn't see Mark. It was nice to get some fresh air and take our minds off things for a while. Captain Yasbrough also wrote Mark a note.

Mark,

Just your company stopping by to see you and to tell you I'm concerned and you're showing everyone here how tough you are, civilian doctors included, and to show that us SEALs are a different breed and mentally stronger than most. I know you'll pull through this and surprise us all. Know I think of you and I will do my best to keep everyone up and positive. I'll stop every now and then and see you and I know you'll pull through.

Captain Yasbrough

And Jacki wrote her own note:

Mark,

I let all of your buddies write in here yesterday. I was too upset to write because you didn't wake up yet and that is crucial. Mom and Micki and I are basket cases. We tried so hard to get you to wake up last night and today. So many from your team came last night and yesterday. Everyone loves you so much. Mark, every friend you ever had has been here. Please wake up Mark. I love you so much. Your body is doing good.

So far you have a good heart rate, good vital signs, no brain swelling. But you are not waking up and we don't know how long you are going to take. Please don't take too long. You're torturing us by taking so long. We know your brain needs to heal before it can work, but you are not moving—you're not giving us a sign. Mark, please give us a sign. Mom can't take it, Micki can't take it and I can't take it. We open your eyes and you look so blank and you don't respond to us. We have tried to yell and talk loudly to you and I even sang to you.

You have to wake up, Mark. We don't want you to be a zombie. We want to hear you sing and see you jump and hear your jokes and stories and have Christmas dinner with you.

Please come back,

And then it was the 22nd. Five days had passed and Mark hadn't come out of his coma. This was Jacki's entry for that day:

Mark,

Mom woke up at four a.m. and was crying for you. It's so bad for her.

She's holding up pretty well but we all have our terrible moments. I went for a long walk with Michele and I couldn't stop crying for you. We don't know if you'll ever come out of your coma or how you will be. It's too much to bear sometimes.

At seven a.m. we tried to get the nurse to let us see you before the surgery on your hand. It's hard to believe that they're going to put you to sleep when you are already in a coma, but they don't want you in pain while they operate.

Each morning when we wake up our only thoughts are of coming here to see you and we write and talk about you in the meantime. Eva bought you a tape player last night and this morning we played Sting for you. Mom and Micki held your hand and caressed and kissed you constantly. We want you to wake up so badly. All of your friends brought pictures and medallions and Bill wrote you a beautiful poem which I will read to you when you wake up.

At eleven-thirty you're going to have surgery to repair your damaged hand. You broke all the bones in the top of your left hand and your thumb bone was out of your skin. They didn't want to repair it until you woke up, but you didn't wake up and they are afraid that it will get infected so now they will operate on you. It's torture seeing all of your injuries.

Last night a doctor showed us all of your x-rays. You have a broken pelvis, broken ankle, smashed hand, brain damage, your lungs are bruised, you're in a coma...but you are alive.

You have so much to overcome. We pray for you and cry for you everyday. We love you. Please get better.

Everyone who came to see Mark felt the same way. We all loved him so much. I realized what a special person my son was, as well as how important it was for him to recover.

I was touched, too, that my friends Josie and Bob from Palm Springs flew in to see him. It was such a joy to see them and be comforted by them. When Josie went into Mark's room, she had Jacki write down what she said:

Hi Mark,

Sorry that you can't talk to me but I will be back. It's great to see your family. They love you and are so fond of you. I want to offer to take you on a plane trip and you get to choose the destination. I'm putting it in writing so you can hold me to it. I know you heard me and I want you to realize I'm serious, so hurry up before I change my mind. I'll be praying for you.

By the 24th of May, Mark hadn't come out of the coma and I didn't know if he would ever make that trip. The trauma doctor briefly met with us in the hall and said that he doubted that Mark would ever wake up and reiterated that the longer he stayed in a coma, the less his chances of waking.

Meanwhile, Mark had his left hand operated on. To see him go through any procedure was a source of despair for us. We were always afraid that something more would happen. It seemed that he was holding our hands tighter, but it also seemed he did that when he was in pain. When they put a permanent tracheotomy in his neck, it seemed he was going to choke. Blood was running down his neck and Jacki and I panicked, but he was okay. It was torture, though, to watch everything that was going on with him. He'd had a slight fever and they'd put him on antibiotics, but they also said it was normal to have a fever with the surgery he'd had. His blood pressure kept jumping higher and that was a worry too.

By the sixth day, Mark still hadn't awakened. I only lived for the moments that I could be close to him. The rest of the time I felt like a robot. They had taken him out of the trauma ICU—which meant we could see him for more than five minutes out of every hour. But they discovered that his fever was a result of pneumonia—and again the fear of losing him gripped me. They told us not to try to wake him up anymore, but we could talk to him softly.

We tried to organize our thoughts. Michele was working on making long-term plans, since we now knew that Mark's ordeal would be a lengthy one. He had already been in surgery twice: first to repair his hand and arm and then to insert a Greenfield Filter in his vena cava to prevent blood clots from traveling. He had a fractured pelvis and left hip, but no surgery was planned to fix it.

The orthopedist was somewhat indecisive about whether or not to pin his hip. He told us he would pin it if Mark was going to run again, but said the chances of that happening were pretty remote. We disagreed, because we didn't want to believe he would never run again, but the thought of his having still another lengthy surgery was too much for all of us, so we told the doctor that we didn't want him to have the operation.

As Mark's officers had promised, I was given a room in the visitor's quarters at the Coronado base, where I would stay until a room came available at a place called Banister House, which was located a block from the hospital. The house had been donated by a wealthy man whose wife had been a patient at UCSD. The families of patients at the hospital could stay there as long as they needed to, but it was hard to get in. It was located on top of a hill where the building overlooked the city. There was a large bulletin board in the entry with photos of many patients and families who had made it through difficult times.

Meanwhile, Bill stayed by our side at the hospital and it was great having him with us. After all, Mark's family consisted of four women, and having a man around was wonderful. I really appreciated it and so did my daughters. I think Eva appreciated it, too.

Mark's doctors kept us updated on his condition. He had different specialists for each injury: one for his broken arm, one for his hand, one for the brain injury and another for his hip. We briefly met with the trauma team doctor in the hall that day. Michele would explain what we did not understand about the procedures and treatments that needed a consent. No matter how we felt about each other, it was clear that Mark's welfare and recovery came first, and Eva, Mark's sisters and I always agreed on any procedures he was to have. Then they got to the point at which they told us that they had done everything they could, and asked us to come the next morning for a meeting with all the doctors.

When that morning arrived we went to the hospital and restlessly waited for the prognosis. Bill came, too. It was interesting that the hospital staff still believed he was Mark's brother. He certainly acted like a brother, and like a son to me also. I was so surprised when I went to pay my bill for my stay at the Banister House, and they told me that my son Bill had already paid it. I felt so fortunate to have my daughters and Bill. I hoped one day Mark would know the love he inspired.

We went into a conference room with the doctors from neurology and orthopedics, a social worker, and I think a discharge planner. The neurologist said that they had done all they could do for Mark in ICU. When I asked if Mark would ever wake up, he said yes he would, but he did not know what level of awake he would be. He added that the fact he was alive after what he had been through was remarkable. I hated the doctor for not telling me everything I wanted to hear, just like I had hated the doctor who told me Allan was dead. Eva said, "Well, I know Mark would never want to be a vegetable, so I hope the family will agree with me if it comes to that." I couldn't even answer her. She had no idea how hard I would fight for my son's life. I reminded her that they had also told us that his brain was going to swell, but it never did. Still, I knew that in our innermost thoughts, each of us was wondering what would happen if what she said came to pass.

I felt such despair, but when we came out of the meeting, Michele said, "We can't give up on him! He would never give up on one of us!" Our pain was great. Bill reminded us that they didn't know Mark or what a fighter he was, and we hung onto each other's hope.

The next day they put Mark in a room where there would only be one nurse for two beds. According to the doctors, his life wasn't in danger anymore. It concerned me that he would no longer be on a monitor, even though it had frightened me whenever its alarms sounded. But the nurse assured me that he'd be in good hands and said that he no longer needed to have three nurses. He was breathing without a ventilator and his condition was no longer critical. I was with him when they rolled his bed into the new room. They were pushing him down the hall, when all of a sudden he opened his eyes real wide and looked straight up at the ceiling. It was the first time since the accident that I had seen his eyes open and it petrified me to see such a blank, expressionless look. I asked the nurse what was happening and she told me he was just in a vegetative state.

It seemed like every hour was filled with both hope and despair—hope that something good would happen, and despair when it didn't. His blood pressure was our latest concern, because it went up and down constantly, depending upon how much pain Mark was in, and he was only permitted morphine every four hours at that point. Whenever he was in pain, he would perspire. So, Bill bought a small fan for him and we put it at the head of the bed to try to keep him cool.

Several days passed and then Mark began to move his right arm. Soon it was in constant motion, back and forth, up and down. His left hand was in a cast, so all we could see were the tips of his fingers. It amazed me that his face was still beautiful, and when he wasn't in pain, he even looked calm. The swelling had gone down quite a bit, and since his more serious injuries were hidden from our eyes, he looked like he was in a restful sleep.

Michele, Jacki, Eva, Bill and I began visiting in shifts. Eva went back to her classes at UCSD. She only had another month left, so she would stay at the hospital until noon and then go to school. We would take over at that point and stay until five, and then she'd return in the evening.

Michele was preparing to go back to Michigan, but planned to return in two weeks. Jacki had another week of vacation and would stay with me. Then she, too, would come back from Florida and stay with Mark while I went back to Michigan to get all the things I would need for an extended stay.

By this time I was obsessed with being by Mark's side. If the hospital had let me, I would have stayed for forty-eight hours without sleep. However, we were taking turns in the room, arranging it so Mark wouldn't be alone for even a minute. Michele showed me how to bathe him, and there were times when the nurses didn't make their rounds quickly enough and I took care of that. I often thought that any mother with a child in Mark's condition would gladly exchange places; would give their life to have their child healthy again. And that's the way I felt. *Why can't it be me?* I asked over and over again. But all I could do was hold his hand and softly tell him, "Hang on, Mark. Hang on."

The time came for Michele to return home and it was very painful, but we promised to call each other every day. Then it was Jacki's turn to leave, and I was alone with Mark, Bill and Eva. I know that even though she had been a nurse for twenty years and was experienced in seeing such tragedies, Michele had gone home with a broken heart. Jacki was sad and upset and I was still in shock from watching my son—that beautiful, wonderful man, lying there with his halo, his tattered arm and hand, and his leg in traction, not able to move anything but his right arm in a bed that was rotating back and forth with that trach. tube in his neck and all the sounds and smells of the hospital. Whenever I left, I felt like I had no home. I went to the Coronado base and didn't even know where I was. And it didn't matter. All I cared about was being near Mark. The rest of the time was of no consequence to me.

Bill had brought a tape player and some cassettes to the hospital so Mark could hear some of his favorite music. Visitors were still coming to see him whenever they had a chance, but one of the SEALs told me that the jump team had to leave. They didn't want to go, and promised me they would be back as soon as they had completed their duties. The day before they left, they all came to the hospital, spent a few minutes with Mark and said their farewells to us. Their bond with Mark was strong. Having to leave without their fallen teammate was painful to them, and every show of their concern was precious to me. I was going to miss their life force.

THE SUMMER OF EL NIÑO

I watched Mark like a hawk. I watched everything that every nurse and every doctor did to him. The man who had put him in a halo was the same person who had invented it. He told me that Mark should never be moved by anyone and that the jacket that was bracing the halo should never be touched. He said that he should be called first if either of these situations became necessary, even if they wanted to take an x-ray or move him in his bed. I was always so afraid that someone was going to make a mistake. Already Mark had been given a shot that he was allergic to and which caused his face to swell. I noticed it right away and they came and changed his medication. I reflected on some of the times I'd spent in hospitals and recalled some of the errors that had been made with me, so I was aware that a mistake could happen and I used that cognizance in my vigil to keep my son safe.

I would get to the hospital at five o'clock in the morning and stay until Eva came, which was around noon. She would stay for two hours and then she'd go to her classes. Then I would again sit at Mark's side from two until about five or six, or whenever it was that Eva returned. She would then stay a few more hours with him, sitting by his side until she was convinced that he'd be good for the night. Then the routine would start over again the next day.

When I came in at five in the morning, I'd give Mark his bath and make sure that he was alright before asking the nurses to give me a rundown on how he was doing. Then I would softly talk to him, always beginning with, "good morning, darling. How do you feel today? You're going to be okay and I love you very much." At times I would vary my conversation. I would often say things like, "I know you're going to come back out of this. I know you're in a sleep and I hope you have good dreams, but please, Mark…come out of it soon." I wished it was like in the movies where someone in a coma would suddenly look at you and say, "Where am I?—and suddenly everything is fine. But deep down, I knew that it wouldn't be like that. Each day I thought that maybe he had moved his toe or some other part of his body or blinked his eyes on command. That's what the doctors said was important—that these moves had to correspond with a command. There are involuntary twitches and nerve-stimulated reactions that occur and those couldn't be mistaken as a sign of him waking up, but if he would move as a result of a command, then we had our sign. Each day I hoped that it would be the day that he would respond.

Jacki was supposed to come back in two weeks and stay with Mark until I came back from Michigan. There I would gather the things that I'd need for an extended stay and pack them in my car so that Bill could pick it up and drive it to San Diego. But, until I actually left, I couldn't even think of that moment. I couldn't think of leaving him for even twenty-four hours. All I could hope was that he would be awake by the time I returned.

One evening as I was getting dressed to leave, Eva, who had just arrived, started to cry. I felt sorry for her. She was showing the cumulative effect of seeing Mark in the same condition every day. "He's never going to wake up," she sobbed.

I took her arm and said, "Please don't cry." I was really touched by her tears and I thought that our common struggle was beginning to bring us closer together. "He's going to be okay," I told her. "He's strong-willed—and he's going to prove everybody wrong and come out of this."

I think I made her feel a little better, but as I was saying this to her, I wasn't sure it was true. I cried when I got back to the hotel as I recalled the fact that I had actually doubted my own words.

The next day they put a tube into Mark's stomach so he could be fed. The procedure was more than I expected. First they made a hole in his abdomen and fed the tube down through it. There was a camera attached to the tube and they had a monitor next to him so they could see where the tube was going. Both Eva and I were there as they were doing this. As we were watching, I grabbed her by the arm as I had done the night before and suddenly the other Eva was beside me. "If you can't take it, get out of here," she said tersely. I was shocked, but I was still learning that one day she could be fine and the next she could be a completely different person. I could never figure out what I was doing that would set her off.

At that point she was beginning to get to me again with her curt words and with her terrible attitude, and it bothered me that she'd never mentioned that there was a problem between her and Mark before the accident. She didn't know that he'd told me that he was going to leave her; yet, the times that she seemed upset about his condition were enough for me to think that perhaps she'd changed. I still felt it wasn't the time to say anything, but the ups and downs were becoming harder to take. Many times I went home wanting to strangle her. Sometimes I'd feel sorry for her because she was upset about her husband, and sometimes I was furious with her because she was so mean to me. I couldn't believe that she could dwell on some little thing that I might have done when Mark was in such a dire condition, and she didn't seem to consider that I, too, was worried sick about him. I noticed that she was acting this way with a lot of people and I could assume that her temper was what put the edge between her and Mark. He was someone who was always in a good mood—life was fun to him—and to have someone who was constantly shifting moods must have been a terrible thing to tolerate. Still, I was trying to be as civil as I could; after all, she was his wife. As hard as it was to hold my temper, I didn't say anything. As long as I was able to be next to my son I would be okay.

Bill still came every day. Sometimes he'd come in the morning and sometimes he'd come in the afternoon. He was trying to be fair and spend some time with both Eva and me. It was always good to see him. His fiancée, Sandy, was an assistant for an ophthalmologist and she would give Bill eye drops to bring for Mark, whose eyes were dry from not being able to blink.

Even though there were so many things to do, I began to call the nurses less, as long as Mark was not in pain. I took on many of the responsibilities of caring for him, although most of the nurses were very obliging and anxious to help Mark. I was always surprised to hear them come in and call him Mr. Colburn, as if he was aware of their presence. They would say, "Mr. Colburn, we're coming to do this for you." Of course, there was never any response.

The hours turned to days and the days to weeks. Under normal circumstances, Mark would have been transferred to a navy hospital, but the doctors promised us that they would not release him unless they thought he was going to be okay. We felt that he was in good hands at UCSD and were content to leave him there as long as necessary.

A short while later I got a call from the people at the Banister House; they finally had a room available for me. There was no food allowed in the room but they had a kitchen that we could use. They also had a washer and dryer available. I would get up at four-thirty in the morning and get ready before taking my one-block walk to the hospital. I'd go through the side door and up the stairs to Mark's room, making sure that I was there when the doctors made their rounds. I always wanted to know exactly what was going on with him.

Soon, Mark was moved again, this time into a room with four beds and two nurses. A couple of beds were occupied by prisoners from the jail. One of them had been stabbed and the other man was ill, and there was a guard posted at the door to keep an eye on them. Sometimes the patients would get out of bed and the nurses would come in and yell at them. I noticed that whenever this happened, Mark's hand would twitch as if he couldn't take the noise. We'd been told by the doctor that he needed a quiet and calm environment. When Eva came that evening, I told her what was happening, and she was more than happy to go to the head nurse and chastise her. I have to admit, she was very handy in that sort of situation. After that, anytime something went wrong, Eva would take care of the problem, since I never had the heart to scold nurses myself.

One of the prisoners was handcuffed to the bed. He would watch me and listen as I talked to Mark. One day he said to me, "Listen, I've been watching you and I want to tell you that I've done a lot of bad things in my life, but I never had someone to encourage me the way you do with your son. I want to tell you that I know—I know for sure—that your son is going to be okay." I don't know why, but it made me feel so good that someone who was in such a desperate situation could give me hope, and I went over and took his handcuffed hand and thanked him.

Eva, Michele and I got to the point where we felt that staying in the four-bed room was not in Mark's best interest, due to all the activity, and we persuaded the doctors into putting him into a private room. Every time he was moved it was a task because of all the presents and cards and balloons he had accumulated, along with pictures of him. We took all of this to his new room and began to put everything back. The shirt Mark was wearing when he was injured had been cut off his body. I took it and finished cutting it so that it would lie flat before hanging it on the wall. Michele had bought him a stuffed Kermit the Frog since SEALs are also frogmen, and we put it on top of his traction pole on his bed, where he'd be able to see it if he woke up. Before the accident, Mark and his SEAL teammates had visited one of the San Diego public schools, first doing a jump and then speaking to the students. When the students heard of the accident they made a get-well banner for Mark, signed by all of them along with their thoughts and prayers, and they had one of the SEALs bring it to the hospital. We hung it on the wall in front of him.

I knew all the nurses from all the shifts, when they came and when they left. Many of them didn't know a lot about brain injuries. They just followed the doctor's orders. But there were a couple who had dealt with them in the past and they were always giving me hope by telling me about their previous experiences. Bill gathered some information about brain injuries, comas and vegetative states from the internet and he brought it in for me. Some of the information was confusing, but I took hope from one thing in particular; if Mark could respond to a command, just as the doctor had said, it would be a very good sign. If that happened, there'd be hope that he could be rehabilitated. It seemed so far fetched when you looked at him though. He was so still. I was worried about those involuntary hand movements as well. I tried to understand how his brain injury kept him asleep, but could let him twitch like that. In the meantime, all we could do was talk to him. Sometimes when I held his hand I would say, "Feel this life! Feel this life, Mark! I'm passing on this life to you. Please feel my faith in you and my faith in God. Please come back. You have a whole life in front of you."

At Banister House, I met many other people with a family member in the hospital. We talked about our loved ones and there was a lot of faith amongst us. There were Arabs, Jews, African-Americans and Caucasians, all living together with one common hope that someone we loved would recover.

Even though I was going to be seventy in October, I was still learning so many things about life. First and foremost I learned that I had much more strength than I had thought. There was an African-American woman who had a baby who'd been born at five-and-a-half months. The doctors had told her that her baby was weak and couldn't be breast fed. Each day she'd tell me, "I know he could if they'd let me try." Then one day she said, "Guess what! I took the baby when they weren't looking and put him to my breast and fed him myself. I didn't listen to the doctors I didn't listen to the nurses, and now my baby will be all right." Another woman had a husband who had undergone heart and kidney transplants and she would always refer to him as *My Honey*. She would say, "I'm going to see my honey now," or "I have to get up early tomorrow because I have to see my honey." Everybody would tell me that they'd pray for Mark. Their prayers may have been Muslim, Jewish or Christian, but we all prayed for the same reason—for the people we loved.

On the day that Jacki came back, Eva was nice enough to pick her up at the airport while I stayed at the hospital with Mark. It was late in the evening when the two of them arrived. When Jacki came into the room, she was clearly shocked at Mark's appearance. He'd lost quite a bit of weight, his face was thin, and he had developed atrophy from his lack of movement, so his muscles were thin too. Jacki went up to him and took his hand, but I sensed something in Eva—a resentment of some sort—so I suggested that perhaps Eva should have some time alone with Mark since she hadn't been with him all day. I tried to get Jacki to come with me to the Banister House, but Jacki said, "I didn't fly all this way just to be with him for five minutes." Since I felt weary and exhausted, I decided to go back myself, hoping that my worry about Eva and Jacki was for nothing.

Jacki followed me ten minutes later, her face red with fury. Eva had yelled at her, telling her to leave the room. Jacki said, "I have never seen anyone behave this way, she was screaming across his bed at me. What is going on?"

I told her that I was trying to warn her, saying that I had to live with her impossible disposition everyday. I said that I try to pacify her and that she would have to do the same, for her brother's sake. I worried about leaving Jacki and Eva while I went home. Eva would have someone new to take out her frustrations on, and Jacki would stand up to her and never back down. So far, I had not responded to Eva's moods, but I knew it wouldn't be the same with my daughter. What a nightmare, I thought. Eva reminded me of the story of Don Quixote, who was fighting the windmills, thinking they were monsters.

The next morning Jacki and I went to the hospital and I filled her in on my routine, which included leaving when Eva arrived. She assured me that everything would be okay and, against my better judgment, I returned to Michigan. I was heartbroken to have to leave Mark and I was worried about the relationship between Jacki and Eva. Jacki didn't have my patience and she was already upset. But I also knew that she would do everything possible for the sake of her brother.

Back in Michigan, I assembled everything I'd need for my extended stay and packed it in the car. Michele thought I needed rest and tried to coax me into staying an extra day, but there was no way I would agree. I had to leave again in the morning. And although it was hard to be back in Michigan, it was nice to see my grandchildren. With all that had been on my mind, I found that I'd missed them more than I realized and it was great to hold them in my arms. I asked the youngest boy, Ryder, how his mother was and he said, "My mother's very sad. She always has tears in her eyes." I said goodbye to them and left for San Diego the next morning.

I took a cab to the Banister House, put my suitcase in the room, then ran—actually ran—to Mark's room. Jacki was there. Mark looked all right, the same as he had when I left, and nothing had happened to him while I was gone, but Jacki was in an uproar. She said, "I'll never talk to that woman again."

I asked her what was going on and she said, "Mark was in pain so I asked the nurse if he could get something for it, so she gave him a shot—and you know very well that she wouldn't have done it unless it was time to give him a shot. Then Eva burst into the room and said that the shot could've killed him and blamed me for it. Then, when I was putting Vaseline on his feet, just as the nurse had told me to do, Eva walked in and said, "Don't touch him! What are you doing? It's disgusting."

The more I listened to Jacki, the more I realized the extent of Eva's problem. She wouldn't let anybody touch Mark and she was probably very jealous of Jacki.

When Eva came to the hospital that night I tried to talk to her, but she gave me a whole list of reasons why Jacki shouldn't be there at all. She told me that

Mark's blood pressure went up when his sister was with him and that Jacki made him nervous. She added that she had tried to kill him. I looked at her in what-are-you-talking-about fashion and said, "Listen...there is no way that anyone is going to give him a shot before it's time." Then, I left my anger at that and tried to calm her down.

When I got back to the Banister House, I told Jacki, "She's his wife. We're going to have to try to be more patient. I don't know what's going on with her and I don't know why she's so angry all the time, but she does have a problem and that scares me."

Jacki stayed two more days before going back to Florida, staying at the hospital with Mark when Eva was not there and leaving when she arrived. I couldn't wait until the following week when Michele would return.

Bill was leery of Eva, too. He knew that she didn't like him and he was afraid that if he said something wrong she'd use her power as Mark's wife and tell the hospital that he wasn't to be allowed to go into the room. Sometimes I wondered if it was possible that Eva didn't know that Mark was going to leave her, particularly since he had apparently told so many people. Yet, when she talked about their relationship she acted like they were the most loving couple that one had ever seen. I think the thing that had bothered Mark the most was when she told him that she wouldn't have another child because she didn't think he'd be a good father. That had really hurt him because Mark *was* going to be a good father, just as Allan had been a good father to him. But now she was coming to the hospital and staying with him and showing concern for him and doing all the things that she had to do. She'd taken care of all the bureaucracy of the hospital stay and had convinced the navy to let him stay where he was. She was determined and never backed down from pursuing Mark's needs.

One morning I came in and Mark's trach. tube was emitting a terrible odor. I called the nurse, and when they gave him a blood test, they found out that he had a staph. infection. Until the infection was cured, we had to wash our hands before we went into the room and the nurses had to wear gloves. For a while, no one was permitted to see him except his immediate family. The doctor said that it would take at least two weeks before he got over it, but about four days later the antibiotics had worked and he was much better. I was amazed at Mark's strength and at how much abuse his body seemed able to endure.

Michele came back and it was great to have her in San Diego again. Immediately she became an effective intermediary between Eva and myself. She also had the ability to calm Eva down and explain things to her. Eva would even confide in her and tell her all her fears. Michele tried to explain Eva to me, but it was hard for me to comprehend. I could only look at her and shake my head, thinking, *You can say what you want, but I have my own opinion.* In a way I wished that Mark hadn't told me that he wanted to leave her. It would have made things so much simpler for me.

Eva didn't reserve her bad temper for us. I had plenty of opportunities to observe her mood shifts. It would always start with that unbelievable look. If it was a pretty nurse who was assigned to Mark, she'd get the look. Then after that day, she'd no longer be assigned to him. I had learned not to complain too much about anybody, because if I did, Eva would run out of the room, go to the head nurse and make a big deal out of it. Sometimes it was okay because the person was really screwing up, but most of the time it was just an issue of minor importance.

Every nasty thing that can happen to someone who's in a coma happened to Mark. He had allergic reactions to medication, his blood pressure would be terribly high at times. He had a staph infection, and then his halo began to slip. They had to call that wonderful man who'd invented it to take the jacket off. I recalled him telling me that Mark's break was so close to his spinal cord that it was crucial that they have five nurses and two doctors there to support him properly while putting the halo on. He came and they began to fix it. They had to go through the whole procedure again and it was torture to watch them unscrew this device from his head, then after the adjustment, screw it back in again. I noticed that while they were doing this, Mark was making faces, which he'd never done before. It was like he could feel what they were doing. Afterwards, I noticed the same grimaces whenever they came to clean his trach. tube. The nurse would come in and say, "Mr. Colburn, we're going to clean out your trach. now," and he would make a face before she even got close to him. *Could it be possible that he was hearing this?* I wondered.

When the doctor came in the next morning I told him what I had seen and asked him, "Is it possible?" The neurologist shook his head and said, "Mrs. Colburn, it has to be in direct response to a command." Nevertheless, he went into the room and asked Mark, "Can you move your toes?" And again, "Can you move your toes? Can you open your eyes?" But there was no response.

It came to the point where the doctors tried to avoid me. One doctor who came into the room while I was there was an intern. He said, "If there had been any kind of a sign I'd put it on my report, but there's nothing." Still, I persisted. I told him that when Mark's SEAL teammates used to talk to him loudly, I'd see some kind of reaction. The intern just looked at me as if I were crazy. The nurses believed me though and said that sometimes a family member would see something that a doctor doesn't see. They told me not to lose hope. Still, every time I thought there might be a sign of consciousness he'd go back to sleep and the routine would continue.

When Michele was there, she'd force me to stay at the Banister House in the evenings and then she'd do the same for Eva the next day. She was worried about me. I told her, "I don't know what's going to happen, but I know that I have more strength than I've ever had before. After this ordeal is over, I may collapse, but until then I'm going to be so strong that you won't believe it." She said, "I believe you, Mom, because I think I'd be the same if this had happened to one of my children."

So Michele left and Eva and I kept our vigils. Two months had passed and Eva appeared to be calmer. When she came in, I would give her an update and then leave immediately, and she would do the same when I came. In a way it was a shame because I knew she was alone, and as far as I knew she didn't have anyone to confide in. I received a lot of comfort from talking to my friends and family and I often thought that it was too bad that she couldn't do the same.

Mark's SEAL teammates were back from their duty and they were again coming in to see him. They'd take turns talking to him, saying things like, "Hey Mark, the surf is up and we're going out. It's the summer of El Niño and the surfing is great," or, "Mark, are you in a green room? Come out of there. Are you in a green room?" It stayed with me—him being in a green room. I could picture him in that green room, riding the biggest wave I had ever seen, and him surfing through but not coming out yet. Many times I'd say to him also, "Are you in a green room, Mark? The sun is shining and the sand is warm, so come out of your green room and talk to us."

One night I went home and couldn't sleep. I prayed and prayed that Mark would be well again. The next morning I went to his room and I put my head on his shoulder and I prayed, "Please, God, I'm not going to make any promises to you because I never keep them. I'm not going to ask you with the stipulation of doing something in return, I'm just going to ask you…give me my son back. Please, God, give me my son back!"

I was in despair. I could think of no other way that he'd ever get better than to ask God. I started to cry and cry. One of the nurses heard me and came into the room and she said, "Mrs. Colburn, don't cry. Your son is looking at you."

I didn't bring my head up because I didn't believe her. I sniffled and said, "No, he's not," and she said, "Yes, I'm telling you—your son is looking at you!" I looked up and I saw that one of his eyes was open and he was looking right at me! I grabbed his hand tighter and looked at him again and I could tell that there was a look of recognition there. She called the other nurse, who said to me, "All right, let me talk to him." Stopping the bed from going back and forth, she leaned over so that she was right over his face and said, "Mark! Open your eyes Mark! Open your eyes!" And to my surprise Mark again opened his one eye. Then she said, "Mark, if you can hear me, blink your eye," and he blinked his eye. Then she said, "Mark, move your toes," and repeated, "Mark, move your toes." We waited and waited and the nurse said, "We have to wait because it takes time for the brain signals to travel in these situations." But sure enough, after a couple minutes Mark's toes began to move.

The room was filled with tears. The nurse told me that she was putting what had happened in her report and that it was definitely a sign. Mark went back to sleep, but we were so overjoyed. I couldn't believe it and I thanked God with all my heart and soul. I called Eva to tell her what had happened. She was thrilled, and anxious to see Mark do something too, and wished she had been there. Then I called Michele and I called her husband, too. I called Jacki and my niece in France—I called everyone. It was such a joyful moment.

The doctors came in and said that the nurse had told them that there was a sign that Mark was responding, and I said, "Yes there was." He tried to get Mark to do it again. He didn't, but I said, "Now you will believe me. I knew that something was happening."

My hope that day was boundless. My prayers were being answered.

THE RE-ENTRY

To me, what had happened was nothing short of a miracle, even though there was no other sign for several days. The doctor told me that, if it really had been a signal that Mark was coming around, his blood pressure would go up—and sure enough, his blood pressure went sky-high. At times it seemed that his arm was going back and forth a little faster, too. I couldn't wait for him to do more, but for two days it was like nothing had ever happened and I wondered if these signs had just been random. The nurse kept encouraging me, saying, "No, it wasn't an accident. It *did* happen and it's going to happen again."

I went to a bakery and bought a sheet cake and took it to the Banister House where I put it in the kitchen with a note that said, *My son opened his eyes today!* I received congratulations from everyone and I thanked all for their prayers.

Eva was getting upset because Mark was more active in the morning, and now that she was done with classes for the summer, she wanted my shift. She had called Michele and told her this. Michele had suggested a new schedule that would appease both of us—and Eva and I agreed to it. Now, Eva would come in at one o'clock and stay for twenty-four hours. Then I would come in and do the same. This new schedule worked out very well for both of us.

I was so happy with Mark's progress. It was such a small step, but a giant one as far as the big picture was concerned. Then two days later, he opened his other eye. And so it went. One day he would show us signs and the next day he wouldn't. There were days when his blood pressure was so high that we didn't ask him to do anything, but we were elated by the progress that was being made, however slight it might have been.

Bill called from Hawaii on the day of his wedding to tell us that they had toasted to Mark's health at the reception. I gave him the good news that at times Mark was opening his eyes, and that made Bill's day complete. They came back the next day, passing on a honeymoon so Bill could be at his "brother's" side.

The time came for us to look for a rehabilitation center for Mark, even though he was only responding to a few simple commands. They gave us the names of three centers, two in La Jolla and one near La Mesa. We didn't know which one would be the best for Mark. I asked one of the nurses and she said the one near

La Mesa was the most highly recommended, but we decided to go and see all of them. So the next morning we went to check them out. Bill offered to take Eva and me, and for the first time since the accident, we left Mark alone.

Our first stop was in La Jolla. As we walked through the center, we thought the rooms were really dark. Furthermore, there was a woman yelling for help from a nurse. Many of the patients looked like they were dying and by the time we got out I was so depressed that I felt I was about to die. My heart sank at the thought of my son being in such a place. While Bill was trying to console me, Eva, who had not said much, said, "Well you knew that this could happen when he joined the SEALs." I was again shocked by her bluntness and said, "Eva, nobody knows if and when these things are going to happen."

We went to the second rehab center. It was a big improvement; it was more like a hospital, and we had a tour from someone who worked there. The physical therapy rooms and lobby were spacious and clean. I felt better about putting Mark in there, but we still had one more to see. Our last stop was at the San Diego Rehab Institute (SDRI) near La Mesa, and as soon as we walked through the door I knew that it would be the place we'd choose. It was clean and brightly lit. We met the doctor who was in charge, a Dr. Stone, a man who projected a combination of youthful energy and intelligence that gave me a world of confidence in him. By the time we finished speaking to the physical therapists, we all agreed that this was the place for Mark. We went back to the hospital and Bill and I waited while Eva filled out the necessary paperwork for Mark's transfer. It was quite a bit more expensive than the Navy had expected; consequently, there were a lot of forms that had to be filled out before they allowed him to be transferred.

Before Mark left the hospital, the doctors wanted to take one final x-ray of his back. I was there when two men brought a portable x-ray machine into the room, and the technician began to open the jacket that supported Mark's halo. I stopped him and said, "The medical person who put this on said not to let anybody remove it unless he was there. Let me have him paged before you do anything."

The technician responded by assuring me that he knew what he was doing. But I went in front of Mark's bed and said, "No, don't you dare touch him. You're not doing anything until he comes." The technician protested to the nurse, but she said that since I didn't want them to do anything until the medical person got there, they had better wait.

About a half-hour later the medical engineer came and thanked me. "I'm glad you called me because this can't be done with two men," he said. "It's too dangerous." He went on to summon three nurses and the man with the x-ray technician and they opened Mark's jacket and held him while they took the x-ray. Once again, I realized how important it was to have one of us with him at all times.

In the interim, the rehab center sent someone to the hospital to begin working with Mark. The doctor said it was all right for him to begin physical therapy as long as he was wearing the jacket and halo. He added that his neck was healing well, but that it would be another two months before the halo could come off. They decided to start the rehab by making Mark sit upright. It was such an unbelievable task. He was so limp that it took three people to position him. Still, it was wonderful to see such a sign of progress.

The next day came and I stayed a little longer than usual because Mark was about to sit up on the edge of the bed. I'd been there since noon the day before and was supposed to leave at noon, but Eva called and said she had a lot of things to sort out with the navy and that she wouldn't be at the hospital till five o'clock. When she got there they were still working with Mark, getting him out of bed and preparing to have him sit on the edge of the bed. The nurses were all in the room watching this, as was I. Suddenly Eva said, "There're too many people here. I want to be alone with my husband." So the nurses left, but I stayed because I wanted to see my son sit for the first time since the accident. I couldn't imagine anybody telling me to leave when Mark was about to have such a breakthrough. But to my surprise, after the others had left, Eva turned and repeated, "I want to be alone with my husband! I think that you should leave!" I felt my face heat up; I was so upset. I walked out and stopped at the door, watching until my son was finally sitting. Then I stormed my way back to the Banister House. I couldn't sleep all night, I was so upset with Eva, and I knew I was going to explode. I knew that this time she had gone too far.

The next day when I arrived at the hospital I called her out of Mark's room and told her I wanted to talk to her. She came out into the hall and I said, "Don't you *ever* try to throw me out of my son's room! And whenever he has a procedure or is doing something for the first time, I'm going to be there." Before I finished—and I was waiting for this—she said, "Well, I'm his wife and I have legal authority."

That was when I exploded. "You know what you can do with your legal authority?" I said. "My son told me that he was going to leave you and I know all the problems he had with you—so don't tell me about your legal authority!"

She looked shocked. "How did you know that?" she demanded.

"Because he told me," I said. Then I turned and walked out.

By the time I got to the Banister House, part of me regretted telling her that I knew about Mark's plans to leave, but part of me felt relieved and I realized that telling her off was the only way to deal with her. I had taken a lot of abuse from Eva. She had insulted my daughter and caused problems for everyone who crossed her path and I was tired of it.

As it turned out, Eva called others to find out if there was any truth to my statement. She called Michele and asked, "Did you know that your brother was going to leave me?" Even though she now knew, Michele told her truthfully that *Mark* had never told *her* that he wanted to leave. When Bill found out that Eva had been told this, he was very uneasy and asked what would happen next. I told him, "Nothing's going to happen. But if she wants to fight with me, then she's going to find the most unbelievable opponent that she's encountered in her entire life."

Michele suggested that I stop in and see one of the counselors at the hospital, and told me that family conflicts often occur when a loved one has a lengthy recovery. I was in such despair that I agreed to it. Between worrying about Mark and putting up with Eva's antics, it was getting to be too much. Unfortunately, my counselor was much too young to understand the complexities of the situation. Even though she was very nice to me, basically, she listened but didn't offer any advice and I soon abandoned that venture.

On the lighter side of things, I found some of Mark's friends very interesting. I especially remember a visit by one of his karate friends. He turned to me and said, "This is going to sound strange, but I know Mark will like to hear it." Then he turned back to Mark and said, "Little Grasshopper...get centered, Little Grasshopper." As I was laughing he said to me, "Mark used to do this all the time. It's from the show *Kung Fu.*" Also, some of the SEALs would remind Mark of some of the funny things that he'd done on their deployments. They'd talk to him like he could understand what they were saying and they would be thrilled when he opened his eyes. I remember one SEAL in particular who broke into tears, then turned to me and said, "If you ever tell him that I cried while I held his hand you know I'm going to kill you." I laughed and said, "No, no...not a word from me." It was amazing to see men who were so feared by others, being so human with their teammate.

The rehab therapist came every day to get Mark out of bed and have him sit for five minutes, either at the edge of the bed or in a wheelchair. It was a pitiful sight. The only thing that held his head upright was the halo and the rest of his body was so limp that he had to be held to keep him from falling to one side or the other. He was so skinny that it was scary. His eyes were slightly open, but his stare was blank. Sometimes they'd sit him on the bed and have him try to balance himself, but after a few seconds he would fall. After these five-minute sessions, Mark would go back into the complete stillness we called his green room.

One day Dr. Stone from the SDRI came to visit. I remember it was a Monday, because this was also a very good day. He told me that he couldn't wait to have Mark at the center and he asked me to show him what he could do. We went to the bed and I said, "Open your eye, Mark," and he opened that one eye. Then I asked, "Can you blink your eye, Mark?" and he blinked it for us. Then Dr. Stone said, "Can you move your toes, Mark?" and actually it only took a short while this time for him to move his toes. Dr. Stone said to me, "This is pretty fast." I asked, "Is it?" and he replied, "Oh yes. I'll tell you, Mrs. Colburn, ultimately Mark will be able to dress himself, eat by himself and be able to talk." I asked him if he was sure and he told me, "Yes, absolutely...and maybe more. I've had many of these cases. All that's required is for him to be awake for a ten-minute period before he's eligible for rehab." I think I gave him a hug; I was so overjoyed.

Michele came back for another five-day stint and we went to find an apartment for me near the SDRI. After we had inspected three or four different places, she told me that my lack of interest was unbelievable. "I'm talking to you and you're not even paying attention," she told me. I guess I was still only focused on everything that was happening with Mark. The apartment that we eventually found was about a mile away. But now that I had my car, the distance didn't matter as much. It was nice, clean and very adequate for my needs. The place wouldn't be available for three weeks, however, and I would have to leave the Banister House as soon as Mark left the hospital. I had to make plans to stay in a hotel in the interim. It didn't matter, though. If I had had to sleep in my car I would have.

In the meantime, as we were waiting for Mark to be transferred, Eva was becoming more and more aggravated. Since she hardly spoke to me at this point, I depended on Michele for any comment from her.

The doctors visited Mark much more often now, and his progress was the talk of the hospital. The staff from the trauma unit where Mark had originally been came in to congratulate us, too. Everybody was talking about the man who had fallen three-thousand feet and was now starting to show signs of life.

But I was wondering how much life Mark was going to have. Even though Dr. Stone's words had opened the door to wonderful possibilities, I still had some doubt. I had put my hope in the hands of God since the time when Mark wasn't given much of a chance. What else could I have done but believe that God would help us? Mark's body continued to heal. The two vertebrae in his neck that he'd broken were healed and we were just waiting for the halo to come off. It was reasonable to assume now that, even if Mark did not regain consciousness, he might be himself again physically.

The navy took its time in having Mark transferred; both Eva and the hospital had to keep pushing them. First, they lost his papers. Then they found them. Then they were going to approve his stay in rehab. Then they weren't. But despite all the hassles, arrangements were finally made for an ambulance to pick him up the next morning. Michele was still with us and Eva was always in a better mood when she was around. I think that she had a calming effect on both of us.

It was decided that I'd go in the ambulance with Mark and they'd follow in their cars—Eva in hers and Michele in mine. Both cars were filled with all the cards, gifts and paraphernalia that Mark had accumulated over the past several months. While we were riding, for a fleeting moment, Mark's eyes were wide open and he was looking at everything. For the first time since the accident, I felt like I could actually communicate with him and I said, "Don't worry, Mark. You're in an ambulance. We're taking you to another place where they can help you rehabilitate." I held his hand—that constantly moving hand—and tried to comfort him.

When we arrived at the rehab hospital, Mark was given a nice room with a big window. They put him in a bed that was stationary, not constantly moving back and forth like the one at UCSD. A nurse came in, and even though Mark had gone back into his sleep, she spoke to him, saying, "Mr. Colburn, I'm going to give you a bell. When you need us, you can just squeeze it and we'll be in right away." She took the buzzer and put it in his right hand—the one that was moving all the time—and we started to laugh because we knew she was going to be back every five minutes. And sure enough, a few seconds later she was back in the room and said, "Can I help you, Mr. Colburn?" We explained the involuntary motion to her. She laughed and put the buzzer on the other side. I told her that I didn't think he'd be ringing the bell and suggested that she stop by whenever she felt it was time to check on him.

That same day, a couple of nurses put Mark in a wheelchair for five minutes. When I think back, I remember it was always such a sad sight, seeing him in that chair.

The next day would mark the start of the actual therapy. In preparation for this, they put him on a special mattress which had been inflated with warm air. When Dr. Stone came in to see Mark, he asked us all sorts of questions and requested that we bring in some clothes for him to wear, as they planned to begin to get him dressed soon. Then he looked Mark over and prescribed his medication.

The time came for Michele to leave again and I drove her to the airport. Even though she knew that her brother was in good hands, her heart was clearly heavy at the thought of leaving him. The future was still uncertain; all we knew was that he had made some progress, but we realized that he had a long way to go. I thought about my youngest grandson and how he would once again see his mother return with sadness in her eyes.

Bill came to visit the next morning. He, too, was anxious to see Mark begin his therapy. Around ten o'clock, two therapists, one of them a very good looking blonde girl, came into the room. There was another bed in the room and Bill, Eva and I sat on it, watching as they worked with Mark. The blonde therapist said, "Mark, we're going to get you up now, so try to open your eyes. We're going to sit you up, Mark. You had an accident and now you're in rehab and we're going to help you." As she spoke, she gently stroked his chest. "We're going to put some clothes on you," she told him as they dressed him, and I could tell it was a difficult process. After about five minutes she said, "That's enough for today." By the time Mark was lying down again, he was perspiring and looked exhausted. This time his eyes had only opened about halfway, however, the therapist told us that he had done very well.

"I can assure you that she's not going to be here tomorrow. She's too pretty," Bill told me when we left, and sure enough, the next day the beautiful blonde nurse had been replaced by a man. We didn't say anything, but Eva quickly explained that she thought that a man would be more effective than a woman. Bill shot me a glance and we had to fight to keep from laughing. It turned out that the man was actually very skillful and just as nice to Mark as the woman had been. Still, it was amazing that Bill had actually predicted this.

Each day began by getting Mark's clothes on. Then the therapists would move and massage his legs and sit him in the wheelchair. Mark looked as if he were a puppet. They would hold him under his arms and put him in a chair, then talk softly to him and tell him where he was. Then an occupational therapist would come and talk to him from one side of the bed, before going around to the other side to try to make his eyes follow her. "Try to make him look from one side to the other," she told us. "Since his right eye is a little stronger, you should stand to the left of him and try to make him look at you with that eye." On the wall was a chalkboard on which Mark's accomplishments for the day were written. That chalkboard became a measuring stick of his progress, and a beacon of hope for us.

We followed all the directions, but it was like caring for an infant.

OUT OF THE GREEN ROOM

Before Michele had returned home, we had a meeting with everyone who was involved in Mark's recovery: the doctor; the therapists, (Don and Nancy); the account representative and the nurses. They informed us that they'd have a meeting every Tuesday at three o'clock, at which time everyone would review Mark's progress, as well as what they expected of him in the future.

In the meantime, his therapy continued. Don and Nancy, working as a team, would always begin by saying, "Mark, you had an accident and you're in a hospital, but you're going to be alright and we're going to help you." Then they'd present whoever was in the room to him to let him know that he had support from his family. When that was done, they'd begin the task of hoisting him into an upright position. I remember the first time they had him stand. He looked so feeble that I doubted that he would ever really get better. He reminded me of the people I'd seen in France who had been freed from concentration camps. He was a very skinny, weak man who couldn't walk on his own and had to be fastened into his wheelchair. After they dressed him, they'd hold him under his arms to balance him, before pushing one of his feet in front of the other in step-like fashion.

When Mark was back in his bed, he would just lie there, not able to move by himself. He would still open his eye every now and then, and when he did, he had the look of someone who was cognizant of everything around him. However, that awareness would soon subside and turn into that blank look that we had become all too familiar with. When he opened both of his eyes, they were so crossed that I wondered if he could see us at all. Whenever his eyes were open, I continued to move from one side of the bed to the other to make him follow my motion. Also, they were beginning to wean him from his medication, except for the pill for his blood pressure.

Mark progressed slowly. He seemed to be more alert, but the progress was painstaking and at times hard to recognize. In fact, often I thought that I was just imagining that his condition was improving, but Don said that he was sitting on the bed in better fashion, that he'd begun to balance himself with one arm as he sat, and that he was aware of his role in the rehabilitation. However, he seldom seemed to recognize anyone and he didn't seem to know where he was.

The second meeting with the doctor and the staff wasn't very encouraging. One of Mark's eyes wasn't responding at all, his reflexes were still very slow and his strength didn't seem to be increasing. About three times a day Dr. Stone would come into the room and look at him. There was never a time that he wasn't available to us. Whenever I called the desk and asked for him, he would come immediately. He was very generous with his time and sometimes he would just sit and talk with me. It was such a change from UCSD, where I couldn't get any answers.

One day when Dr. Stone was standing beside Mark's bed, Mark opened his eyes real wide, and he stared fixedly at the ceiling as though he were in a trance. My legs started to shake. I thought he was dead. Dr. Stone grabbed him by the chest and shook him until he came out of it. I asked him what had happened and he said that he wasn't sure, but it might have been a seizure, and added that even if it had been, it was nothing that would kill him. Still, I noted that he looked concerned. As for me, I had to sit down and regain my composure. I really had thought the end had come.

Mark's teammates still visited on a regular basis. Two or three would come in every day—sometimes in the morning, sometimes in the afternoon—and Dr. Stone was fascinated by them. He would ask them questions about Mark, and of course they'd tell him all sorts of stories about him and the things he used to do. One story in particular sticks in my mind. They told him how Mark had fallen thirty feet out of a helicopter and landed on a cement surface because the line he was holding hadn't been secured. They all thought he was seriously hurt, but he got right up, brushed himself off and walked away. They told the doctor that after that, they thought Mark to be indestructible.

I had finally moved into my new apartment. It was convenient because I only had a five-minute drive to the rehab center. Even when I wasn't with Mark, it made me feel good to be that close to him. The apartment itself was adequate and in a good neighborhood. Michele had made sure of that.

Mark still had the trach. in his neck and he still had that frightened look whenever the nurses came in to clean it. I always felt especially sorry for him when they did that procedure, and I could understand that look because it must have been painful. But the fact that he was frightened as soon as they told him what they were about to do assured me that something in his mind was working. He also seemed to be more active in his bed. Every once in a while he'd turn to one side or the other and it was wonderful to see his body getting some life back into it. His eyes seemed to follow motion a bit faster, even though eventually the blank, vegetative look would return. He probably had cramps in his legs because they would frequently twitch and he would raise one of them, which he couldn't have done before. I'd take that leg, feel for the cramp and massage it until it loosened up. I kept doing this, and I soon noticed that, whenever I came into the room, he would position his leg so I could massage it—another sign that he was aware of what was going on around him.

Once a day the nurses would put him in a wheelchair for me and I'd take him out on the terrace. I thought that a little fresh air would be good for both him and me. His face bore a strange expression, as though he were in pain, but when I asked Dr. Stone about this, he said that the contortions were a result of his brain injury. Nonetheless, it was hard to look at him. Even in the hospital I observed people trying to avoid eye contact because he looked so frightening. Sometimes on the way out to the terrace, I'd see our reflection in the glass—me pushing my debilitated son in his wheelchair—and my heart would break. I didn't think he was ever going to get better. The poor man, sitting in that chair, wincing at the light, was nothing of what he used to be. Still, I'd take him out, give him a couple of breaths of fresh air and then bring him back to the room.

At one of the Tuesday meetings the staff told us to bring in pictures of Mark. They said that, when he woke up, they could trigger some memories. So the next day I brought some pictures to the rehab, pictures from when he was a little boy, some of him and his sisters, and one of him and his dog, Wellington. Eva brought in some pictures of her and Mark when they were in Guam. As I sat in his room looking at the photographs, I wondered how much, if anything, he would remember when he was fully conscious again. The progress he made was so slow that it seemed imperceptible. Most of the time when he sat upright, both of his eyes remained closed. In a way it seemed like he was an infant and that he had to learn everything, just as an infant would.

I was always amazed by the patience and kindness of Mark's therapists. They'd tell him where he was and what had happened to him, and they would go on to tell him what he'd eventually be able to do. Mark had always responded to kindness and love and I knew that his was exactly what he needed.

Every time someone would come and visit him for the first time, be it a friend of mine or of his, I could see the look on their face as they tried to contain their emotion. It was shocking to see him in this shape and I could see it in their eyes.

It was now three-and-a-half months since the accident. Dr. Stone said that Mark would have to go back to the hospital to see if the halo was ready to come off. His body was healing tremendously well, much better than anybody had ever expected. And although he was supposed to keep the halo on for longer than four months, after his examination at UCSD, the doctors decided that it could be removed in another two weeks. The very thought of not having that awful halo screwed to my son's head, along with the jacket that I knew must be so hot and uncomfortable, was such a relief.

I was with him when the doctor took the halo off. Mark sat in a chair as they unscrewed it. As they lifted it off, my joy turned to horror as his head dropped forward and his chin went down into his chest. It was a relief when the nurse put a soft collar around his neck to help support his head. As a little time passed I realized that it was still an improvement, and as they put him back in his bed, it was wonderful to see his head actually resting on a pillow for the first time in four months. His hand was still in a cast and they decided that when he was further into his recovery, he should have more surgery. He was cooperating with us now when we changed his bedding, moving to one side and then to the other when I asked him to. Sometimes when I did this, he'd put his good arm around my neck and it seemed that he was trying to hug me. Dr. Stone also said that the trach. tube could come out since Mark's breathing was better. Now that he was moving around, there was less danger of him developing pneumonia.

As Don and Nancy continued to work with Mark, it became clear that he was making progress step by step, both figuratively and literally. With their help, he'd take three steps one day, then four the next. When his energy waned, his right arm would become more active and he'd put on a leave-me-alone expression. It definitely looked like he wasn't enjoying the rehab; yet, as slow as the progress was, it still offered us hope.

I noticed now that, whenever one of his SEAL friends came, Mark would open his eyes a little wider. Something about them, perhaps their hearty voices, seemed to trigger something in him. I filled the room with cookies and candy so they'd feel welcome whenever they came. Captain Yasbrough, whom we hadn't seen since Mark moved into the rehab, came in one day with another SEAL who was being transferred to Florida and wanted to see Mark before he left. When he bent down over the bed, a strange thing happened; Mark started looking at the trident on his shoulder. No one can wear a trident unless he is a SEAL. It's something they're all very proud of. So he was looking at this pin, which has a eagle looking down, and he wasn't taking his eyes off of it. It was the first time since the accident that he was so focused on any one particular thing. We all noticed it. Captain Yasbrough turned to me and said, "My God, I think he knows what he's seeing. Either he remembers what it is, or he's trying hard to remember...his look is so intense." The two SEALs visited with my son and then left, but an hour later the young man who had been with Captain Yasbrough returned to the room with a huge, wood-carved trident. He said, "Captain Yasbrough had this on the wall in his office and he wants Mark to have it." And, taking a chair, he stood on it to nail the trident on the wall in front of Mark's bed. I was so touched by the gesture.

Eva continued to be the same; her behavior was unpredictable. One day she'd be almost nice, and the next she'd be in a different mood. I went to see the hospital's counselor to help me face some of my fears. "If Mark gets better," I told her, "Eva's never going to let me see him." I went on to explain everything about our situation, including how Mark had planned to leave Eva. I also told her about my concern about the long-term care of a brain-injured patient—how the caregiver has to be strong and how Eva had openly admitted that she was not equipped for the task. The woman tried to reassure me. She also tossed out the fact that most marriages don't last when a husband or a wife suffers a brain injury, and that I should at least be prepared for that. She told me that Eva probably had fears, too, mainly that Mark wouldn't recognize her; that it'd be easier for him to remember his distant past than the things that happened in the most recent years. I told her that, since it was so hard for me to deal with Eva, I had resolved not to deal with her, but instead, to simply be with my son as much as possible.

Meanwhile, Mark seemed to be more active everyday. In fact, Dr. Stone said that if he moved too much they'd have to put him in a different bed. I didn't know what he was talking about; I could only picture a bed with rails. One day when I came into the room I found Eva in tears. "Mark tried to get out of bed," she told me, "so I went to get the nurse. When I returned he'd fallen out of bed and onto his back." She was crying and I felt sorry for her, but I felt worse about the fact that Mark had fallen and I asked her, "Why didn't you ring for the nurse instead of leaving him alone?" She said, "I didn't think he would actually get out. When I saw him put one foot over the other I thought that was as far as he would go. I went to look at him and he seemed fine."

She paused and I saw her expression change. "Something else happened," she said slowly. "When Dr. Stone came in to look at him he asked Mark if he had hurt himself, and Mark looked at him and whispered, 'No.' "What?" I exclaimed!

"Yes," Eva told me as though she could hardly believe it herself. "He said his first word. And when Dr. Stone asked him if he wanted to go back to his bed he said, 'Yes.' It was barely audible, but he still spoke. The doctor asked if we'd heard him say anything before and I told him that this was a first."

I was filled with mixed emotion. I was elated that Mark had spoken, but I was also concerned about the fall. I was afraid of what they'd have to do to restrain him, to keep him safe. But as it turned out, Dr. Stone had him put in a Craig bed, which looked like a little house on the floor without a roof. It was about eight-by-eight, with a door that locked, and the inside walls were padded. It was large enough so that we could go in and sit with Mark on the mattress, but we had to be sure to lock the door after we came out. At first I thought it was frightening—but everything that was happening to him was frightening. However, he seemed to be calmer when he was inside that bed. Also, the walls blocked the light that bothered him so much.

I was so glad that he'd said a few words; I hadn't heard his voice in so long. But he didn't speak again for many days and I wondered if those words had been a freak occurrence, something that would never happen again.

Soon, Mark began to move around in the bed, rocking side to side on his back to the point where his knees were raw from rubbing against the sheets. I asked the nurse for a foam mattress to put on top of his bed for a little added cushion. This, along with the bandages they put on his legs, seemed to help, and within two days, he entered what Dr. Stone called the *agitated state*. He explained that that was the natural progression from the vegetative state, and he arranged for Eva and me to watch a video that showed different people going through that stage. It was not a pretty thing to see and I thought to myself, *Mark will never get to be like that*. But unfortunately, he did. I asked how long that phase would last, but Dr. Stone couldn't give me a time frame. He just said that we had to do our best to keep him from becoming agitated, to keep the shades drawn, and have his visitors be as quiet as possible.

Eva and I continued on a schedule at Mark's side. Switching in the afternoon, we would spend twenty-four hours on and twenty-four hours off. I knew that Eva went home sometimes in the middle of the night to feed her bird, so I would often go in then to see if Mark was asleep, then leave before she came back in the morning. Dr. Stone had prescribed a sleeping pill for him since he had started to move around a bit, so on my shift, I would go home in the middle of the night, take a shower and sleep for an hour or two. I tried to time my absence to coincide with his sleeping pill. Many times I thought to myself, what a strange situation this man, my son, is in with his wife. Like a bad soap opera story, he tells me that he's going to get a divorce and the following week he has this tragic accident. Now we don't know if he will remember any of it.

Even when he was asleep, there was a lot of work to be done. Eva and I had taken over most of his care by then. We did his feedings through his stomach tube, during the night and during the day. He had been getting 2000 calories of his liquid nutrition each day and he was still losing weight, so we did two night-time feedings as well. Before I left each day, I would make sure there were clean towels and sheets in the room, and Eva would do the same for me. Since we hardly spoke to each other when we changed shifts, we wrote what we had done and what needed to be done on a dry erase board hanging in the room.

One night the nurse was with me as I was trying to turn him around. Whenever I did anything for Mark I'd always talk to him, and this time I had just said, "Mom's going to turn you around," when I heard him say, "Ma." I looked at the nurse and she beamed, "I heard it!" I began to cry and she did, too. I was so happy to hear his voice for the first time in five months that I couldn't wait to call everybody and tell them what had happened.

Mark's agitation became incredible. Sometimes he'd grab at things without knowing what he was doing. One time, as I was trying to change his sheets, he moved his leg and tripped me so that I fell into a sitting position on the bed. At the same time, he pushed both of his legs toward me, pinning me against the wall with so much force that I thought he was going to crush my chest. Somewhere along the line he had regained a lot of strength. I couldn't believe what was happening. I called out, "Mark! Mark! You're hurting me!" Then slowly he seemed to recognize who I was and he backed off. By the time I came out of his bedroom I was quite shaken.

Once when one of the nurses came in to change the sheets after he had wet the bed, she said, "You're such a bad boy." Mark gave her a dirty look, and every time after that he'd grab her and try to hurt her, but he was too slow. It seemed like he was trying to use one of his karate moves, but in slow motion. One time she came in and he goosed her. She said, "Oh, don't do that. Your wife is going to be mad." Of course Mark didn't know what he was doing, but I still had to laugh.

On another occasion Nancy had Mark sit at the edge of his bed. She was bending down to put his socks on and a pencil fell out of her pocket. When Mark grabbed it, after pausing for a moment, she said, "Mark, here's a piece of paper. You have a pencil. Why don't you write your name?" To our amazement, Mark began writing his name. He wrote a big M and a small A, then a big K and a small R, all the letters of his name. Every time he did something new I would cry, and then I would get on the phone and tell his sisters what he had accomplished.

Jacki was supposed to come back, but it didn't surprise me to learn that Eva had a problem with that. She said that she'd prefer that Jacki didn't come while Mark was in the agitated state because she felt that she'd only make him more nervous. At this point, I agreed, not because I thought that Jacki would aggravate Mark, but because I was worried about her and Eva getting into a fight in front of him. So I called my daughter and asked her to postpone her trip for a month. She was disappointed; after all, she hadn't seen her brother in many weeks, but she agreed to it after I explained my reasoning. I felt bad because she had her vacation time scheduled. Now, when she came, she'd have to miss work.

The therapists were working with Mark in many different areas. Now that the soft collar was taken off, his neck was allowed to move freely. Early each morning, around five, one of the occupational therapists would come and try to show Mark how to brush his teeth and comb his hair. She'd take his hand as she guided him through these tasks. Half the time he seemed aware of what was going on and the other half he seemed to have no clue, but there continued to be no doubt that whenever his SEAL friends were visiting he was the most alert.

One morning when Don and Nancy woke him up for therapy, he turned his back and refused to do anything. They tried to coax him for a while, but then decided just to leave it alone for the time being. The next day the same thing happened. Mark wouldn't get up and he wouldn't turn around. He would just move his right arm and shake it back and forth. Don explained to me that it was very painful for the brain to have to relearn all these tasks and that Mark was in a state of depression, which meant that he wasn't willing to do anything to help himself. It was very alarming to me to have this setback after he had been making so much progress.

One week passed and then another, and still no cooperation by my son. I was getting desperate. Then I told Dr. Stone how Mark seemed to be more responsive whenever his Navy SEAL friends were in the room. I said that, if *they* encouraged him to get up, he would probably do it. He said, "Okay, why don't we try that," and he talked to the physical therapists and told them what they were going to do.

Eva called one of Mark's buddies, and that same day two of the SEALs came in and went over to the bed, opened the little door and said in a forceful voice, "Okay, Mark, let's go. You have to get up and walk. Now!" They pulled him out, and to everyone's delight, he offered none of his usual resistance. They put his clothes on, then each took an arm and guided him all the way to the end of the hall. I was thrilled. It was another good day. From that time on, two SEALs came every day at five o'clock and, along with the therapists, got Mark out of bed and performing his rehab exercises.

It was early September, and it was time for Michele to come back. She was on a schedule at work and at home which allowed her to come to California every three weeks. I called her before she set out and told her that when she arrived, Mark would know who she was. He still had his moments where he'd go back into his own little world, but most of the time now he knew everybody.

When Michele got in, we stopped briefly at my apartment and then went to the hospital. She was going to spend the whole night with Mark so I could stay home for a day, and then do the same for Eva the next day. When she walked into the room and saw him, though, I could see in her eyes that she was frightened by the way Mark looked. I tried to reassure her by telling her that he knew who she was, but she looked at me and said, "Mom, please don't." I went up to him and said, "Mark, where is your sister Michele?" She was standing behind him at the time and he took his finger and pointed her out to me. When he did, both Michele and I were in tears.

That night as I went to sleep in the apartment, I didn't even want to think of what was going to happen next. Everything was so turbulent, fine one minute and not the next. I didn't know what was going to happen and that was so difficult for me. I wondered how much my son would ever be able to enjoy his life. I hated it when I took him outside and he'd start flailing his arm back and forth to keep away from the light. I wondered if he'd ever be able to enjoy the sunshine again. I was constantly bombarded with questions like that. Then, in the middle of the night, I got a call from Michele and she was crying. "Guess what, Mom," she said, "he called me by my name. As clear as could be, he looked at me and whispered my name."

Eva was upset that he hadn't said anything to her yet, but one day when I came in she was sitting at the table with Nancy. Mark was facing her in the wheelchair, and Nancy said, "Mark, tell Eva that you love her." And sure enough, Mark said, "I love you Eva." I was glad to hear that because I wanted him to say something to her. I was afraid that she was going to feel even more resentful toward us if he didn't.

The fact that he had spoken a complete phrase was amazing. After that it seemed that the words really began to flow. That night I heard him say, "Cold…cold," and I put a blanket on him. Then, five minutes later he'd say, "Hot…hot," and I'd take the blanket off. It went that way the rest of the night—hot, cold, hot, cold. The therapists had him speak in phrases, saying, "I'm hot," or "I'm cold." From there he started to name the artists who performed the music we were playing for him. Soon it got to where I could ask him what he wanted to hear. It was great to hear him respond like this. He'd say "J.T." for James Taylor, or "The Beatles," or a specific song by title, like, "Wake up Susie." Then he'd drift back into his green room again, seeming to not know where he was or who was around.

The SEALs continued to work with the therapists. At the end of the hall there was a gym. They began taking Mark there and putting him on a stationary bike.

He'd try to move the pedals for about a minute, which was a long time for him. Then they'd get him down and take him back to the room. They'd also take him to the bathroom before they left. It took a great amount of time and patience just to move him.

In late September, one of his friends, Mark Kurtz, came from Florida to visit. They used to have a band together when they were in high school. Mark Kurtz had been an extra in a few movies in Florida and had gotten a part in a film in which he played a doctor. Anyhow, he came to the hospital dressed from the set, in a white lab coat. He told me that he'd stay with Mark for awhile so I could go home. When I came back, Don was in the room giving Mark Kurtz an update on my son's spinal condition. He was telling him all the details and Mark Kurtz would nod, looking knowledgeable and not saying anything. I started to chuckle and just had to tell Don that Mark wasn't really a doctor, that he was just playing the part in a movie. Don laughed and said, "Well, it doesn't surprise me. All Mark's friends are crazy." And later, when Mark Kurtz came back from the cafeteria, he told me, "They didn't let me pay for my lunch because they thought I was on staff." I assured him that I'd tell Mark all about this episode as soon as he was able to understand. Mark stayed with my son for two days before returning to Florida.

In the meantime, my Mark was becoming more and more vocal, and along with that he began to say quite terrible things, which was also something that the doctors had told us would happen. During the meeting that day, they told us that whenever he'd say anything vulgar we'd have to tell him that it wasn't appropriate. I spoke up and said, "I've only heard my son say a few words in the last five months. Do you think I'm going to tell him that there are words he can't say? As far as I'm concerned, at this point, he can say anything he wants." They all looked at me like I was crazy, but I didn't care. That's the way I felt.

Soon enough, though, I was sorry that I'd been that adamant. The nurse who was always getting on his nerves took the brunt of the new abuse. He'd tell her to get the hell out as soon as she came in. Also, there was another nurse who would always ask, "What's my name, Mr. Colburn?" This time when she asked, Mark answered, "Your name is Mary, you bitch." He loved to be in his Craig bed, but if you stood on the outside and looked down at him he would insult you.

When Bill returned to San Diego, I told him that Mark was speaking. He was thrilled to hear this, but I warned him that if he talked to Mark he'd probably get insulted. He said, "Don't worry, he won't do that to me." So he went to see Mark. He put his head over the top of the bed, looked down and said, "Hey

Mark, I hear you can talk now," and Mark said, "Get the fuck out of here, you spy!" It took Bill about ten minutes to make Mark realize who he was.

One night Mark was going through his hot-cold routine. I had gotten up numerous times, taking the blanket off him, then putting it back on again. Finally, I went up to him and put the blanket on his neck and said, "Hot, cold, hot, cold," and to my surprise and to my joy he started to laugh. It was the first time he'd laughed since the accident and I was so thrilled at that sign that he would be able to enjoy life again. After that I'd play that same game with him, just as if he were a little boy.

There were still times when Mark didn't know who I was. Once in a while he called me Mrs. Colburn, as though I were one of the staff, probably because I had blankets and sheets in my arms much of the time. When he was in a coma I used to softly sing to him, and now, during one of his restless times, I asked if he wanted me to sing to him and he said, "No. Fuck that!" I started to laugh and thought, *Maybe that's why he wasn't coming out of his coma…because I was singing.* I also came to realize that every time I told him I was going to leave he'd get angry and use the 'F' word, so I started posting a note inside his little abode to let him know when I'd be back.

Mark's sense of humor was returning. One day when he was sitting in his wheelchair, a therapist crossed one leg over the other for him, and he looked at everybody and said, "Merv Griffin." Another time I'd taken him for a ride in his wheelchair, and when I asked him if he wanted to go back to the room he mocked my French accent, just as he used to when he would call me Inspector Clouseau, and said, "Back to zee rhume." Still, despite these occasional barbs of humor, he'd return to his green room, that famous green room. I was beginning to realize how hard it had to be to come out of it and face the world.

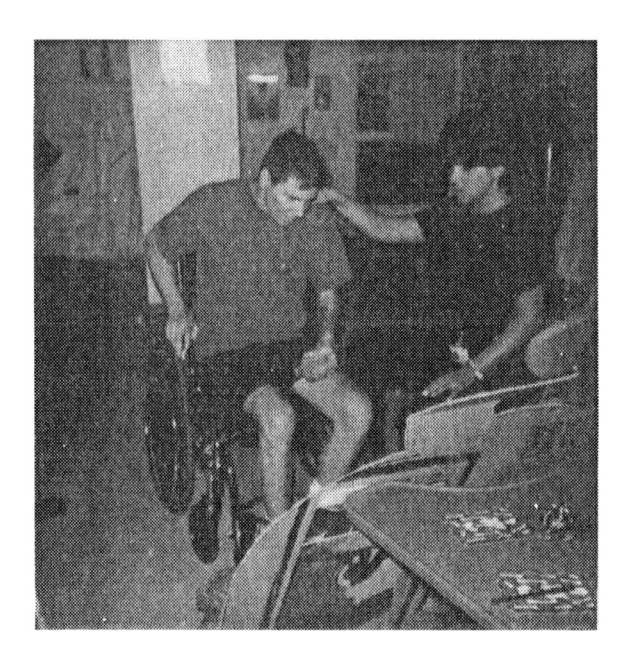

The Tuesday meetings became more exciting. Now that Mark was making progress, there was beginning to be talk of him going home. There were several things he had to learn before that could happen, though, one being how to use the bathroom by himself. In fact, that was the task he had to learn next. We went around the room, and, of course, no one wanted to volunteer, so we all started to laugh. Finally, the task was assigned to his SEAL friend, Jonezy. Nancy was in charge of teaching him how to eat again. I realized that these two tasks were going to take a lot of patience.

Suddenly, it seemed like everything was slowly getting back to some sense of normalcy. As soon as Mark learned to eat, they could remove that unsightly tube that was in his stomach. Even with all the calories that were in his liquid diet he was still losing weight, so the sooner he ate solid food, the better it would be for him. Nancy began by putting a plate of ice chips in front of him and putting some small pieces in his mouth. Then she'd feel his throat to see if he was swallowing and say, "Almost, Mark. Swallow, swallow." It was painful to watch, but she encouraged him by saying that if he could do it, they could remove the tube that he was always trying to pull out, (along with his clothes). Apparently his skin was very sensitive because he couldn't stand to have any clothing on. Teaching him to eat was a long, painstaking task. Not only did he have to relearn how to swallow, but he also had to be able to take the spoon in his hand and bring it to his mouth, which seemed almost impossible. His hand would fall back down, and whoever was feeding him would take the spoon and make him try it again. He still only had the use of his right hand, even though Dr. Stone had taken the bandages off of his left arm and hand. After his initial surgery, shortly after his accident when they tried to put the pieces back together again, his left hand didn't move much and had become atrophied with contractions. The bones were healing, but he would need further surgery to get the use of his hand back.

Then it came time for him to try some different foods. They prepared soup and mixed it with a thickener so he would be able to swallow it easier. Thin liquids were too difficult to swallow at that point. He made slow gains, but the weakness of his hand was apparent when he tried to hold a spoon. It amazed me that the same hand that could throw a urinal across the room couldn't bring a spoon to his mouth!

Mark had been able to use a urinal while in bed for several weeks now, and began calling it his "Piscapo," which later became his "Joe Piscapo." His sense of humor was again intact. After he would use it, not knowing exactly what to do with it but knowing he didn't want it around, he would throw it across the room if no one was watching him. That kind of impulsive behavior happened once in a while, and it was clear that he needed to be watched constantly.

Every move Mark made was slow, but a miracle to me. Because I had never expected him to come out of the vegetative state, every little step—eating, walking, laughing, speaking—excited me. However, my enthusiasm was always tempered by his appearance. He still looked so pitiful. The people who came to see him for the first time were still shocked by the way he looked. I could read it on their faces and it hurt me to see that. When my sister-in-law, Sharon, came from Michigan to visit, she was quite shaken, even though she tried not to show it. Josie and her friend from Palm Springs came several times, and had become used to the way Mark looked. Josie would bring cookies or chocolate, but more important, I appreciated her company. When Mark was asleep we'd go outside the room and talk. It was good for me to be able to talk to a friend.

The day finally came when Mark swallowed some ice chips. Then he did it again the very next day. That was followed by two days where he made no progress but then, on the fifth day, he ate ice chips again. Like every aspect of his recovery, he was making progress, but it was very slow. The next day they prepared some soup with just a little thickness to it and he swallowed that, too.

If Mark was on the floor, he couldn't get up. During therapy with Don one day, Michele and I watched as he rolled from his bed to the floor and started to crawl. I wanted to help him but Don said, "No, let him go." He crawled until he reached a big chair that was in the corner of the room. Grabbing it, he pulled himself up. He didn't stand, but he managed to hoist his butt up off the floor.

As I watched my adult son crawling like a toddler on the floor, my heart would break all over again. At times I couldn't help thinking that it would be impossible for him to have a normal life. I knew he would never be the way he was before the accident, but I hoped that he would be able to at least understand what was going on around him, to be able to stand up on his own, and maybe have a look on his face that would make me believe that his soul was still there. I wanted to wake up one morning and not feel the tremendous sadness I carried with me at all times. Each time he would do one small new thing, I would rejoice, but in the back of my mind I wondered if it was perhaps the last time he would do anything more toward his recovery. Happy moments were fleeting, but I forced myself to never give up hope for continued improvement and better days.

Jacki was ready to come and see her brother again. I went to Eva and told her that Jacki would arrive the next day. I didn't wait for or care to hear any reaction. She was coming and that's all there was to it.

When Jacki came to the hospital the next day, she, like Michele, was a little upset at first to see how emaciated her brother had become. When they stood him up, it was shocking to see his frail, thin body. She was happy, though, to see the progress he had made since her last visit.

She stayed for a couple of days before going to see one of her friends in San Diego. That next day I went to the hospital alone and when Eva came in she immediately told me, "I can tell Jacki made him nervous. I can see it in him already." But I was ready for her. "This is where you're wrong," I said. "Jacki hasn't even been here today. She's been visiting one of her friends in San Diego." I confess that I was glad to have had the opportunity to call her on it.

We got into it again after one of the Tuesday meetings. Dr. Stone had said that Mark was ready to eat solid foods and that he could try anything. I asked if I could bring something in for him and he said, "Certainly. In fact there's a great delicatessen across the street and you could get something for him there." After the meeting Eva approached me and said, "Why do you have to bring something in? The food in the cafeteria is good enough."

Nevertheless, when I went back to the apartment I stopped at the market and bought a chicken to make a chicken soup that I brought in for him the next day. I was very happy to be able to cook for my son again. From then on I'd bring him something to eat everyday. Sometimes I'd get a pie from across the street. Other times I'd bring him soup or scrambled eggs. I noticed that every time I came in with a dish, Eva was more irritated with me, even though she didn't say a word;

her facial expressions were always a dead giveaway. Finally, one day she said, "Well he's going to have to get used to this hospital food." My thinking was that, since we wanted him to be released as soon as possible, there was no reason for him to get "used" to the hospital food. However, to avoid a quarrel, I began to put the food I brought in the refrigerator in the kitchen, only giving it to Mark after she left.

DESPAIR, HOPE AND FAITH

There was no doubt that my son was making progress, but he still continued to slip back into his green room from time to time, and I cherished those moments when I could have him with me. His appetite improved and I continued to bring him food every day. I remember one morning, I sat down on one side of his Craig bed and began to change the sheets, as he slept on the other side. While I was doing this, he turned so that his head rested on my right arm. Then he opened his eyes and bit me. I could tell that he couldn't recognize me by the glazed look that he had. I couldn't get him to open his mouth. His teeth were clenched tightly and I was in excruciating pain. I tried pleading with him, telling him who I was and how much it hurt until he finally appeared to recognize me and let go. The pain was tremendous and I could see his teeth marks embedded in my flesh.

Since he had never done this before, I was more worried about his behavior than the actual biting. The first thing I did was to find Nancy and warn her about this. However, as she was feeding him just a short time later, Mark bit hard on the plastic spoon and broke it. She had to reach into his mouth to get it. I thought he was going to bite her finger off before she could get the spoon out. We decided to let him rest for awhile and see if he was more responsive later in the day. Meanwhile, my arm turned a deep black-and-blue and Nancy had the nurse come in to look at it. She told me that Mark wasn't biting intentionally, but that it was simply a reaction. I understood. Mark had never said a harsh word to me in his life. Again, I worried about what would happen if he didn't progress any further. What if he stayed the way he was now for the rest of his life?

But I knew that he was recognizing us more and more often. Certainly, he knew who the Navy SEALs were. Among them he had his favorites, like Charlie and Jonezy, who sometimes would bring his little boy. Regardless of which of them came, Mark was at his best when they were around, perhaps because he'd spent the last eight years with them and they were fresh in his memory. He knew their voices and they were like brothers.

One day as Eva and I were getting ready to switch shifts, a small, intense-looking man whom neither of us had seen before entered the room and introduced himself as The neuro-psychiatrist, a neuro-psychiatrist who would be working with Mark. No one had said anything about a psychiatrist. The neuro-psychiatrist seemed surprised that neither Eva nor I were more curious about his appearance, although, by this time, we were accustomed to new people coming in to do various therapies. He asked us a few questions, then gave us some guidelines to help speed Mark's recovery: keeping the curtains in his room closed, very little noise, and limiting visitors to one at a time. Visitors should be advised to say their name to Mark and remind him who they were, and, when conversing with someone, not to talk about him as if he wasn't there.

The next day as I was sitting alone with Mark, I got a call from Michele. She told me that Eva had complained about me to the neuropsychiatrist, who in turn had said that if Eva and I weren't able to get along, I wouldn't be able to see Mark.

I felt as though I had been stabbed in the heart. "You have to be kidding," I said. "What happened?" Michele told me that Eva had told her that I never listened to anything that she or anybody else said and she told that to the doctor. I was so upset. I thought of the many months I had spent with my son, night and day, putting up with Eva's quirky personality for Mark's sake. I got to the point where I couldn't take it anymore. The weight of the whole ordeal had finally taken its full toll. I felt a despair that I had never felt before. The burden of the situation overwhelmed me.

As a consequence, Michele called the doctor and let him know that I had been with Mark since the accident, and told him that his ultimatum had been issued thoughtlessly and had hurt me very deeply. Later that day, neuro-psychiatrist called me at the apartment. I told him how I felt and let him know how desperate I was. He said he'd make arrangements for Eva and I to meet with a counselor. I told him that I would rather have things continue the way they were, with the two of us having as little contact as possible. I said that Eva and I were so different that there was no way we could ever get together. I did tell him that she was taking good care of my son and that she should be able to see him as much as possible, but that I didn't think that I should be out of the picture, since I was willing to adjust to her schedule.

Still fuming about the allegations Eva had made against me, I called her and said, "How could you complain about me after all the mistakes you made with my son—like when you left him alone and he fell out of bed? If you're trying to drive me away, then think about what you'll tell Mark when he asks what happened to me. He'll know it's your decision because he knows that I'd never leave him on my own accord." In my anger I was unrelenting and she finally hung up on me.

Eva had another meeting with the neuro-psychiatrist and Barbara, the woman to whom we'd spoken with before. She spoke with me alone and then with Eva and me together. We were told that Mark would need the help and support of both of us, along with his sisters and friends and everybody who loved him. I obviously agreed one-hundred percent with this.

"Don't think that I don't appreciate the fact that you spend twelve-hour days with my son," I told Eva, "but you have to understand that just because I'm from another country and have an accent doesn't mean that I think with an accent. I can't have you constantly reminding me of what's good for Mark and what isn't. And I can't constantly deal with your mood shifts. Sometimes I just reach the point where I give up on trying to be nice to you."

To my surprise, she didn't have a negative response to this. I think the fact that I told her that I appreciated the time she spent with Mark had appeased her to some degree.

After the meeting Barbara spoke to me alone and reminded me again that marriages don't always last when someone has a brain injury such as Mark's. I told her I hoped that wouldn't be the case. I'd spent six months with a woman who drove me completely out of my mind, and for her not to stay with my son after all of that would be very sad. I told her my hope that Eva stayed in love with him and that he loved her, too. I added that when he came to, I hoped he'd remember the good in their relationship, not the bad. All I wanted was for them to be happy.

After all the meetings were over, Eva came to me and said she was sorry that she'd given me a hard time. I hugged her and said, "Let's just work together to get Mark well enough to go home." For the first time I felt that we were reaching an understanding and that she was putting forth effort into our relationship.

A few mornings later, I came in and realized that Mark was no longer grimacing as though he was in pain. I thought it must have been because he was getting better, but I found out, at a much later date, that it was because they had given him Botox to relax his facial muscles. I probably would have worried about this if I knew it at the time because Botox doesn't always work. But luckily, the contortion never returned. I noticed, too, that he seemed to be more at ease when I strolled with him in his wheelchair. The sun still seemed to bother him, but his arm wasn't flailing in anger as much as it did before.

At about that time Mark was moved into a very large room, which had a stove and a refrigerator; the room was used for someone who'd be released soon. In order to make the move they had taken his Craig bed apart. When Mark saw them doing this he started to scream and yell in distress. We all tried to calm him, but I thought, *How can he be calm when they're dismantling his safety zone.* He didn't settle down until they took him into his new room and he saw his bed being put back together. I could tell that it was still difficult for him to comprehend things, even relatively minor things. It must have been a nightmare to be in his world, not knowing where he was or what was happening.

Things were going smoothly now between Eva and me and it was so good to be able to have a civilized conversation with her concerning my son. It was the way it should have been all along. Each day Mark grew a little more aware of what was going on around him. Now and then I would still play the hot-cold game with him and it was good to hear him laugh. When the SEALs came they would stay longer and would actually have conversations with Mark about different things that had happened in the past. Eva brought in some video tapes and we all got together, including the doctors and nurses, and we watched film of Mark taken when he was a SEAL. It was good to see clips of his old, humorous, handsome self. Even Mark laughed as he watched. Another time, four of his best friends came in and said, "We ordered a pizza and we're going to share it with Mark." Then they pushed the tables together and put Mark at the end. I left them alone, but watched from the hallway as they ate and laughed. It was so wonderful to see my son having fun again that I was in tears. As they ate, they continued to reminisce about the SEAL days. Then they ran Mark through the events that brought him to a rehab facility, and Mark seemed to fully comprehend what happened.

One night as I was sitting in the room with him, a nurse rushed in, turned the TV on and said, "Something terrible has happened!" She tuned into a news channel and we heard that Princess Diana had been killed in Paris. I was shocked. I looked at Mark and noticed that he was attentively listening. "Do you remember Princess Diana?" I asked him, and he did. I cried for her as I recalled that she was the same age as my son.

At our next Tuesday meeting an announcement was made that Mark would be going home on the seventeenth of October. It was finally here, the day I'd been dreaming about for the past five months and it was so great to think that he'd finally be going home. But at the same time, it was frightening for me, and I suspect for Eva as well. I wondered how I was going to manage. They lived in La Jolla, which was far from my apartment, and a daily commute would be a long one. The staff went on to tell us of the preparations they had to make for Mark's transition. They were going to wake him up more often, and since he still relied on his urinal from time to time, he would have to be weaned from that. I began coaxing him to use the bathroom on his own. I remember trying to pull him out of bed and not being able to do it, and he wasn't strong enough to get up on his own, so I rang the bell to get the nurse. From then on, he'd tell us when he had to go, and that's when we knew he would soon be able to go home.

It so happened that the seventeenth of October was going to be my seventieth birthday, and Mark's thirty-seventh birthday was going to be on the twenty-seventh. I looked toward this as the day I'd get my greatest birthday present. There were still times that I'd look at Mark and think that he wasn't ready to leave the hospital, but I put my faith in the words of the doctors and hoped that when October seventeenth came, he would have made the necessary progress to be allowed to go home.

Four days before he was to be released, at around three or four in the morning, I was at the apartment when I got a phone call from the nurse. She said, "Your son wants you—please come. His wife must have gone home during the night and he woke up alone and now he's hysterical. We tried to calm him, but he's asking for you." I rushed to the hospital and into his room and found Mark out of control. He said, "I had to go to the bathroom and nobody came and I fell down and peed on the floor and I've never been alone before and I don't know why I'm alone and why Eva isn't here. She said she was going to stay with me."

I tried to calm him as much as I could, but particularly since he was no longer in his Craig bed, which had been a comfort zone for him. Finally we got him settled down. I realized he was more alert now and that his sleeping pill did not last through the night. The doctor told us that from then on somebody should be with him all night, every night, which was exactly what I had always done whenever I was on my watch. I had never guessed that Eva would go home. The worst part was that she didn't tell him that she'd be leaving. When Mark was quieter, I called Eva and told her what had happened, but Mark grabbed the phone from me and called her every name in the book. I tried to calm him again and eventually got the phone out of his hands. When I did, I told Eva that it might be a good idea for her to come back to the hospital. After I hung up, Mark continued to vent. All of a sudden, the anger he had towards her was coming back to him. I wanted to calm him down before she arrived, but I had to ask him one question first. "Mark," I said, "when you get out of the hospital, do you want to go home with your wife or do you want to come back to Petoskey and be with your family? Whatever you say is okay and that's what we'll do." And when he told me that he wanted to go home with his wife, I said, "Then calm down. Don't insult her. She didn't tell you that she was going home because she thought you were sleeping, and now she's on her way back here."

I felt a certain relief that he wanted to go home with his wife and figured that, despite his tirade, he had forgotten what had happened before. In the past, Eva had told me that she wanted Mark to come home with her, and that she'd made all the necessary preparations for him. She said that she wanted me to come over as much as I could and assured me that it would be a workable situation. Still, Mark had to be happy.

I knew Eva wanted me to be around to help them, at least for a while longer. I told her that I would be there until both of them were comfortable with their lives. I knew I couldn't stay forever, but I wanted them to know that I intended to come back every month for at least a week to help them. Eva was not working and had not resumed classes at UCSD, so she could just take care of Mark. She planned to go back to school sometime in the future, but we never knew how long Mark's recovery would be.

When Eva and Mark's anniversary arrived, I had the nurses put Mark in his wheelchair and I took him downstairs to the gift shop so he could pick up some flowers to give to his wife. He wasn't totally aware of what was going on, but the physical therapist suggested that I take him there to get Eva something for their anniversary. He figured that this might trigger some memory performing the normal tasks of life. He said to have Mark pay the cashier by himself as well as collect the change. It was noisy when we got down there and I could tell Mark was getting nervous. After being away from people for six months it was probably like being on the moon for him. I pushed him to where they had the flowers and had him select the ones he liked, then took him to the cashier. He paid for the flowers without saying a word. When Eva came to see him, he gave her the flowers, and I think she was genuinely happy about it.

Mark's birthday was coming up, too, so we decided that, when he went home, we'd have a party at their house and invite all the SEALs and his other friends and really make an event out of it. Michele was going to get the drinks and Eva and I would get the cake, while the SEALs' wives were going to bring the food. Making the preparations for a celebration at home seemed wonderful after all the days and nights we had spent in the hospitals, first wondering if he was going to live, if he would come out of his coma, and then how much he'd progress in his recovery. Now everything seemed different, even though he still couldn't walk alone, was terribly underweight, despite gaining ten pounds, and still made occasional trips into the green room.

Shortly before Mark was due to go home, I was informed that crews from the three local television stations and reporters from the press would be covering the event: the story of the man who fell three-thousand feet, lived, and was now well enough to go home. Little did they understand that the road ahead would still be long and difficult for my son, as well as for the rest of us.

Some of the staff had gone to Eva's apartment to help her get things ready for Mark's homecoming. They told her about the things he'd need and pointed out the changes she'd have to make in the apartment. Obviously, he would need wheelchair accessibility, and he would also need handrails by the bathtub and toilet. I told her that I'd stay at the hospital for the final forty-eight hours so she could concentrate on getting everything ready.

I had some tee shirts made for the staff. Each shirt had a Navy SEAL trident on it, along with the person's name. I also had a special one made for Mark that said, **SURVIVOR OF A 3,000 FOOT PARACHUTE FALL.** On the morning of Mark's release, I gave the shirts to everybody: the doctors, nurses, physical and occupational therapists, and I gave Mark his shirt, too. A short while later, reporters and cameramen from all the television stations in the San Diego area arrived at the hospital to interview him, along with the doctors, Eva and me. I had observed my son in front of an audience many times when he had had his band, and now when he was under the lights and they were asking him questions, he really came to life. He was actually being quite the ham. He was also speaking in phrases, as opposed to the one-word responses that he would usually give. It was a pleasure to see him beaming and talking to all these people. Don and Nancy stood behind Mark and helped him walk for the cameras, but they did it in a way that they couldn't be seen and it looked like Mark was walking on his own.

Finally it was time for him to go. Two of the Navy SEALs came and helped us load everything from the room into our cars. Mark got into his wheelchair and went downstairs, where the SEALs helped him into Eva's car. I followed as we all went back to Mark and Eva's apartment. Bill was there when we arrived, brightly clad in an Hawaiian shirt, and he had an identical Hawaiian shirt for Mark to wear. The atmosphere inside the apartment was festive and it was a wonderful moment for all of us. Mark was alive and he had taken another major step. He and Bill were sitting on the couch, laughing, just as they had done when they were boys, and Eva was in a very good mood, too. In fact, she was smiling and looked happy to have Mark home. That day, we all had something to smile about.

The night came to a close, and after helping Mark get in bed, Bill and I left for our respective homes—Bill, back to Encinitas, and I went back to my apartment near the hospital. It was a long ride for me and, as it would happen, I got lost and it took me two hours to get home. In a way that was good because I had a lot of time to think as I drove.

Even though Mark was home now, he had a lot of progress to make. He was still slow with his words. He couldn't get off the couch by himself, and he needed someone to hold him when he walked to his wheelchair. I thank God that Eva was a physically-strong person and was able to help him get up and around. I had decided to give her total autonomy with Mark, particularly now that he was back at their apartment, and I determined to make a point of not doing anything that would get her angry. Being home with his wife was good for him and that was enough for me. It seemed that he still didn't remember anything about his plans to divorce Eva and I was okay with that. In fact, I hoped that their relationship would benefit from having a fresh start. Eva really had showed a lot of devotion to him all the time he was in the hospital, and the way she felt about me wasn't important. She seemed eager to take care of him, so as long as she did that, I was going to do everything in my power to help her.

Mark's birthday party was sensational. Many SEALs and their wives were there, as well as all his other friends, and Jacki and Michele had flown in for it, as well. Even Dr. Stone came. Mark was elated and talked to each and every guest. His friends brought him presents and posters and all the things that he liked. It was a great day for me, just to see my son having a good time. Jacki had brought in the diary that she'd started when Mark was first injured and she presented it to him. When the night came to an end I said goodbye to Mark and promised to take him to the beach the next day.

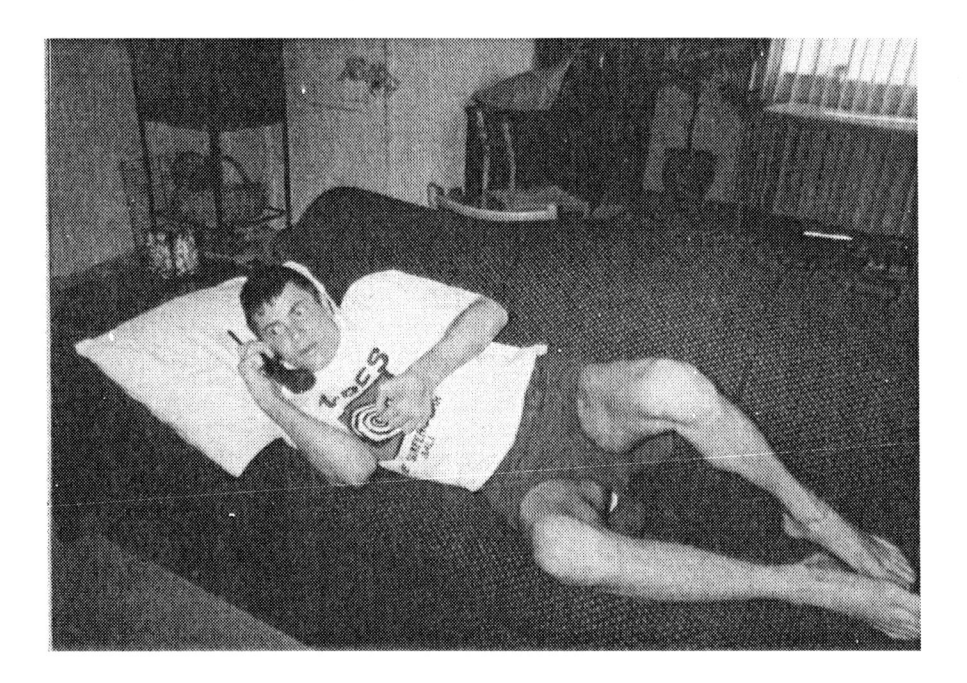

The following morning, Jacki, Michele and I put Mark and his wheelchair in the car and drove a few blocks to a beach called Wind and Sea, one of the places where he used to surf. The wind was blowing briskly, but the sun felt warm on our faces. We couldn't take him down to the sandy beach in his wheelchair, so we sat on a bench just above and watched the waves crash into the shore. It was sad to watch Mark look out at the surfers, when only six months earlier he had been out there himself. Still, it was good to have him outside in the sun and talking to us. We stayed there for a while and took some pictures before taking him back to the apartment.

Just before we went in, Jacki asked, "Did you read any of the diary that I wrote for you?" Mark's face grew angry and he said, "Eva read it to me and she also told me that you tried to kill me and that you touched my injured hand!"

Jacki looked shocked, then started to cry. Clearly, she was devastated. I bent down and looked my son in the eye and said, "Mark, this is your sister, Jacki. Do you think for one minute that she would try to hurt you or kill you? She asked the nurses to give you a shot because you were in pain. I don't know *where* Eva got the idea that she was trying to kill you. Nobody at the hospital would have given you a shot before it was due, regardless of who asked for it."

Mark calmed down and told Jacki that he was sorry. Then I told him that Jacki had never touched his hand, that she only caressed his fingers while he was in a coma. Again, he apologized. I was furious again with Eva for telling him all this, but I had sworn that I would do whatever it took to make the situation work. I felt in a way that I was being blind-sided by this woman and wondered what else she might conjure up to set Mark against us. Saying that about Jacki was so unfair, particularly since Jacki had spent thousands of dollars on all the trips she had made from Florida to San Diego to see her little brother, and she was as worried for him as anyone else. When we got into the house, I took Eva aside, and in as calm a tone as I could muster, I asked her why she would tell Mark such a thing about his sister, especially when such a thing couldn't possibly have happened, and she simply said, "Oh, yeah, I forgot about that."

The only assumption I could make was that she was jealous of the diary Jacki had kept and she wanted to somehow compromise its value. I thought that if she was that jealous then she had to be terribly unhappy, and if that indeed was the case, I hoped that she wouldn't make Mark unhappy, too. Her resentment or dislike for us still seemed intense and I couldn't figure out why. However, I'd been told that a person with a brain injury couldn't deal with a lot of controversy and I wasn't about to do anything that would upset my son, so I said what I needed to say and then I dropped it.

The remaining three days of Jacki and Michele's visit went well. After they left, Eva and I mapped out a routine. I would go to their apartment in the morning, and I would make lunch. We decided to take turns driving Mark to his outpatient appointments. Sometimes I'd take him to the hospital, then Eva would come and get him so I could go home from there, because I lived nearby. In the mornings she'd help Mark take a bath and get dressed, after which he would usually sit on the couch and watch TV, or talk to us, for most of the morning until his physical therapy sessions began. For someone who went through as much as he did, he always seemed to be in a good mood. He was always joking and sometimes he wouldn't stop laughing.

My oldest grandson, Nicholas, was attending school in California, but he had never had the chance to see his uncle. I don't think he wanted to see him the way he was anyway. I don't believe he could have handled it. I remember the first time Nicholas came to California after Mark's accident. I had gone to get him at the airport and taken him out to eat. He was looking at me strangely, I suppose because I had lost a lot of weight and he hadn't seen me looking so rundown before. He said to me, "Nana, you look like Yoda." I started to laugh and told him that that was the way I felt, too. I hadn't seen Nicholas much during that time. He had been busy with his studies, and when he had free time he had spent most of it at the dorm or with his friends. He also understood that I had to devote most of my time to Mark.

Physical therapy was very hard on Mark, both physically and mentally; so difficult in fact that he'd often have to stop in the middle and go to a room and rest before continuing. Then when he got home, he'd go right to bed. When I took him home myself, I'd try to make dinner for the three of us, or I would at least pick up a pie or something to contribute to the meal. Despite the incident that had been triggered by Jacki's diary, Eva was still fairly pleasant with me. She did not go back to school, and was too busy caring for Mark to get a job. Between taking him to doctor appointments and physical therapy and taking care of the many navy issues that constantly needed to be addressed, she didn't have much time for herself either. Taking care of Mark's needs was more than a twenty-four hour job. She knew that she needed me to help with Mark, and was probably being nice to me for the same reasons that I was being nice to her. I loved my son and I wanted to be involved in his life during his recovery, until I knew I wasn't needed anymore.

Mark hated everything that had to be an effort for him, but he continued his therapy by going to a pool once a week. It was a difficult procedure; the therapists had to take him out of his wheelchair and then, holding him under the arms, lower him into the water and make him walk. It was strange to see him in the pool because he was now afraid of water. We're talking about a man who made his living as a Navy SEAL, and someone who once loved to swim and surf and be at the ocean.

I remember one day in particular. The team of therapists brought Mark down to the pool where several other patients were working. Mark began to protest. "No," he said, "I'm not getting in the pool anymore. This is not for me," whereupon all the other patients who were there, people who also had brain injuries, began to protest, too. When Mark saw the effect his words had, he started to laugh. It took the physical therapists a good forty-five minutes before they could get anybody back in the water, including Mark.

When Charlie, one of the SEALs, began to pick him up every week and take him there, Mark would paddle around in the water and sometimes he'd even put his head under, although it was still very difficult for him. The staff thought the pool was great therapy, and I thought it was, too, since the buoyancy of the water helped support Mark's body weight and made it easier for him to stand, and the resistance that the water offered was a good physical exercise for his muscles.

After Mark had been home for three weeks, I told Eva that sooner or later I had to go back home to Michigan. We decided that I would go in the first part of December, and if possible, she and Mark would come to Petoskey for Christmas and spend a week or two at my house. It was a good plan. Mark was excited and Eva seemed to be receptive to the idea as well. So I made plans to fly back home, since Bill and Foot had offered to drive my car back for me. Meanwhile, I continued to make myself as useful as possible, disappearing whenever I felt that Eva wanted her space. Mark was technically still in the navy and they said that Eva would be able to hire someone to help her at the apartment, so I felt better about leaving.

Mark's physical therapy wasn't producing any rapid results, but he was slowly improving. His speech was a little better and he seemed more aware of his surroundings. He continued to have sessions with The neuro-psychiatrist; he enjoyed these meetings and looked forward to them. One day I went to Dr. Stone and said, "You've always been honest with me in the past. Tell me. When do you think Mark will be able to walk by himself and get up by himself?" He told me that we were still two or three months away from being able to do that, but I took encouragement from his words.

Eating was yet another problem. Mark still had trouble swallowing thin liquids. Food would go down very well, but when it came to swallowing a liquid, he had to have thickener put in it to prevent him from choking. Occasionally we'd try to give him a thin liquid to see if he had progressed enough to swallow it on his own, but up to this point he still couldn't do it. It was frightening to see him choke, but the doctor assured me that as long as it wasn't a solid food there was nothing to worry about. He qualified this remark by explaining that the liquid that Mark didn't swallow properly went into his lungs and was absorbed there. We kept trying to give him a little something that he'd have difficulty with every now and then, just to help him practice his swallowing. It seemed for a while like the most common words heard at the apartment were, "Swallow Mark, swallow." We even joked that we should teach Eva's parrot to say the word.

Eva was very good with Mark and I appreciated that a lot. She seemed to want to have him with her and she did all the necessary things, both pleasant and unpleasant, and showed a lot of love for him. She was patient with him and I could tell she was trying hard to be nice to me, too. When I saw this I felt it was okay for me to go home.

The time came in the first part of December. I took Mark to the clinic that day. Eva was coming to pick him up and I intended to follow her home and leave my car at their apartment for Foot to pick up. I had moved out of my apartment and had everything I wanted to take with me packed away in the car. I had given the furniture away to some of the SEALs and was ready to go.

Before Eva arrived at the clinic, I went out and bought a cake for Foot and Sandy, Bill's wife, who were sharing a birthday that day. When we all got back to the apartment I told Mark and Eva about the cake. I didn't realize it, but again I had started something. Mark looked at me and grimaced. "Why are you giving them a cake?" he demanded. "They don't deserve a cake!"

I couldn't understand why he would say such a thing. I reminded him that they were taking my car back to Michigan for me and that they were two of his best friends and that they had been by his side the whole time he was sick.

Mark seemed satisfied, but I knew the culprit. I looked at Eva and said, "But if it's going to bother you, it's okay. You can keep the cake and we won't give them any." I also had a present for them. When they came I met them outside and gave them their gifts so that Eva wouldn't be upset. I realized then and there, though, that she was never going to get over her jealousy of anyone who was close to my son. Of course Mark had acquiesced as soon as I explained things to him and I begged him not to become negative towards people, and he said, "I'm sorry, Mom, you're right."

I had no idea whether Eva was glad that I was going home or if she was going to be bitter because I was leaving Mark alone with her. I still sensed that no matter what I did she was never going to be my friend. Mark didn't feel too bad about my leaving since he knew that he'd see me at Christmas, but it broke my heart to leave him.

I left for home around the tenth of December, seven months after this ordeal had begun. The flight home was a sad one and I spent most of it trying to put everything into perspective. When I got to the house, it was good to see Michele and Dan and my grandchildren. My little dog Maggie wasn't around anymore though. Michele and Dan had kept her at their house with their three dogs, and one day when Dan drove home, Maggie came running out of the woods and onto the driveway. He didn't see her coming toward him and ran over her. I recalled when Michele came out to California and I asked her how Maggie was doing. She said, "She's not doing very well." And when I asked her what she meant, she had said, "Well, she died." I looked at her in shock. She had gone on to explain what had happened, and how she and the kids were so upset that they didn't talk to him for several days after. When Mark had heard this, he had begun to laugh hysterically and wanted to call Dan and say, "Why did you kill my mother's dog?" But he had been laughing so hard that he couldn't do it, so he had Bill call. Dan felt terrible, but Mark and Bill couldn't help teasing him about it.

I felt bad about Maggie, but I didn't want Michele to know. I thought, *My son is alive. How can I feel bad about the dog?* Still, when I came home and she wasn't there to greet me, that's when it really hit me—my little friend of eight years was gone. I still miss her.

I began to look forward to Mark and Eva's Christmas visit. I started getting the house ready for them, as well as getting it decorated for the holidays. I decided, too, that I'd have a banner made that said **WELCOME HOME MARK AND EVA.** I appreciated that Eva was willing to bring Mark to Michigan, particularly since I understood how difficult it would be to travel with him. She said she was going to bring her bird, too. I thought that would make a cumbersome traveling situation even more difficult, but as long as she got here with my son I didn't really care.

Crews from the local television stations planned to be at the house the day after they arrived to cover Mark's homecoming, just as they had done in San Diego. There was no doubt that it was an amazing story, and it was not a surprise that the local media was eager to report it. When they came, Mark was again happy to be in the limelight. They shot film and took pictures and asked him a lot of questions, and he answered in a low voice that you could hardly understand. I was so happy to have him back at the house.

When I had first returned to Petoskey, I had still been terribly depressed. There had been the letdown of not being by my son's side anymore, after caring for him for all those months. I felt a void. Even though I knew he was all right, I was in a very sad emotional state and I would cry for the simplest of reasons because I still believed that everything that had happened in Mark's recovery was a miracle, and I wanted to talk to somebody about it. My first impulse was to go to the Catholic church. They had a pieta that was a reproduction of the one from Italy. I used to always sit by that statue, and I remember that sometimes I would look at the Virgin Mary holding Jesus Christ and think how terrible it must have been for a mother to see her son in such a way. Now I felt a kinship with her because I had experienced it, too. I had seen the Pieta when I was in Italy with my sister and we both admired that piece of work, both for its artistic qualities and for the love that it represented. Now, every time I saw it in this church, it held a meaning to me that it never had before.

I had talked to the pastor, Father Andre. Even though I had attended masses there many times, I had never met him personally. I explained to him what had happened to my son and how I thought it was a miracle. I was crying and crying as I told him everything that had happened during the seven months that I stayed with Mark. He gave me a hug and asked me to bring Mark to the Christmas Eve mass if I could. I came out of the church feeling much better. When Mark and Eva came to Michigan, I asked them to come to the midnight mass with me. However, they were both very tired from the trip, and they promised to go with me on Sunday instead. So I went to midnight mass with my son-in-law, Dan, and one of my grandchildren.

Michele and Dan were going through a difficult time in their marriage. They had been married twenty years, but now they were both unhappy. I never thought something like that could happen to them, and was so sorry because I loved both of them. The combination of this difficulty along with what was going on with Mark made everything more discomforting. Dan decided to come to the church with me that Christmas Eve because he was aware that I thought a miracle had happened with my son, and he thought that it wouldn't hurt to ask for a miracle for him and Michele, too.

So the three of us went to the mass, and as Father Andre was delivering his sermon he said, "This family has been the recipient of a miracle." He held out his hand and pointed us out to the rest of the congregation. "This woman came to me and told me how her son fell three-thousand feet and survived, and now he is back at home with her for the Christmas holiday." Then he asked us (in front of everybody) "Would you come with your family on Sunday?" I shook my head yes. I was terribly emotional, and I thought that he had done such a wonderful thing.

That following Sunday we all went to mass: Mark and Eva, Dan, Michele and their children and myself. I told them, joking, "I thought the only time all of us would be at the church together would be at my funeral." All of our friends from the area came as well, and during the service, Father Andre asked Mark to come to the front and talk to the congregation. We pushed Mark up the aisle and

Father went down to meet him. He asked Mark, "What do you think saved you?" and although Mark wasn't able to speak very well, he replied, "God saved me."

We had a wonderful Christmas and it was good to have most of the family home. Jacki thought that, because of her relationship with Eva, it would be better if she didn't come. It was an unfortunate situation. I told her that she could come out to California for the party we'd throw when Mark would officially be retired from the navy in the spring.

It was hard for me to see them leave, but I knew I'd see Mark again soon. He had to have surgery on his left arm and I told Eva that I'd be there to help her when that occurred. After that, there'd be his retirement ceremony from the navy and they were planning to throw him a big party. When I was near Mark I could tolerate the whole tragedy, but when I was away I found myself very depressed, which was an unusual state for me. I was so depressed that my doctor suggested that I talk to someone, and sent a lady from hospice to come and see me. She told me that I was experiencing the same emotions that one has when they are grieving over a death. She went on to tell me that it was okay to feel that way because in a way I did lose my son; Mark would no longer be the way he was. She came to see me several times and I began to feel a little better. I had had to be so strong while I was with him in California, and now that I didn't have to be a rock, it was bound to be a letdown.

Planning for the trip to California helped me get out of my doldrums. I had reserved a room at a hotel near their apartment and they were going to pick me up at the airport. When I arrived, however, they weren't there. I started to worry and called everyone I could think of, but couldn't reach anyone. Finally, I was paged to the desk where I was told that Eva was coming, but that she'd be late. In fact, it was about an hour and a half before she arrived. She told me that Mark had suddenly experienced some back pain and she had taken him to a doctor. She said that Dr. Walters from the navy had given him an x-ray, and it had turned out that he had pneumonia. She went on to tell me that his surgery would have to be postponed because of this. I felt terrible. We went back to their apartment and I found Mark looking tired and frail. I stayed with them for a while, then went to the hotel. I could tell that Eva was worried about Mark and she told me how she'd been up most of the previous night watching him because he was in pain.

I spent the afternoons with my son while Eva went out to do shopping or errands. She always seemed to have something to do, so we didn't get in each other's way too often. I felt she was uncomfortable when I was hanging around at times, even though she was pleasant. I began to learn the unspoken signs that it was time for me to leave, and I would do just that. We had only one expectation of each other; to take good care of Mark.

Mark's behavior was strange. The pneumonia seemed to make him regress. He slurred his words more, spoke in a low voice, and had lost his sense of humor. You could tell he wasn't feeling well, he spent a lot of time on the couch and was terribly fatigued.

A week later we took him in for another x-ray and it appeared that his pneumonia had cleared up, so his surgery was rescheduled for the following week. The hand surgeon was going to remove the plate from his forearm and operate on his fingers in an attempt to straighten them. Since he was going to be in the hospital for three days, I told Eva that I'd stay with him during the surgery so she could catch up on her rest. Clearly, she would need her strength to care for him when he came home.

The surgery took place later that morning and I waited until Mark came out. I understood that operating on the fingers was a difficult procedure, so I wasn't surprised when the operation took four or five hours. When he came out, a nurse took him to the elevator and Mark said to her, "Are you going to kiss me?" She replied, "No, I don't think it's part of my job." She was a cute girl and I knew that Mark would be saying some funny things to her. Of course he had a lot of drugs in him and because of that and the brain injury he was unpredictable.

When I learned that the hospital only had two private rooms available, and they told me that Mark wouldn't be able to have one because they didn't think he needed his own room, I tried to explain that he still didn't realize where he was or what he was saying half the time and that he might not be the best roommate. But I couldn't sway them. They put him in a room with another patient and he wasn't there two minutes when he yelled at the nurse when she tried to put pillows underneath his arm. Then he started screaming that he didn't want to be in a room with someone else. The head nurse came and immediately agreed to put Mark in a private room. He was still easily rattled at that point and in the phase where he'd say anything at any time to anyone.

Shortly after he arrived in his new room, a nurse came in to give him a shot. But Mark resisted and yelled at her, saying that he didn't want anyone else coming in. When she went to get another nurse, I told Mark that the next nurse would be real pretty. When she came in, Mark yelled, "You said she was going to be pretty and she's not!" I felt terribly embarrassed, but this nurse was able to give him his shot. Dealing with Mark was difficult because one of the effects of his brain injury was blatant honesty. Everything that he thought would come out of his mouth—unfiltered. However, the rest of the night went smoothly and in the morning Eva arrived. Two days later we took Mark home.

Eva and I began getting along unexpectedly well and I was thankful for that. When I'd first arrived I had been surprised to see that she and Mark had bought me a little puppy. It was a Jack Russell terrier and he was adorable. Mark had picked him from the litter because his markings were unique. He called him Bandit, and although he told me I could change the name if I wanted, the name fit him so well that I kept it.

Bandit had two black patches around his eyes and looked like he had a bandit's mask on. Eva and Mark weren't supposed to have pets in their apartment so they had to hide him and make sure he didn't whine or bark. They both were so fond of the little puppy. They had bought a big cage for him to stay in while he was at the apartment, and also a bag for him to stay in on my flight home. Every afternoon and evening Eva would take him for a walk, but then he'd have to return to his cage. He was so small that he wasn't much of a problem, although Mark said that one day he'd grabbed their bird and they thought he would kill it, until they managed to pry his mouth open and get it out. Bandit was such a cute little guy and I thought it was so nice of them to do that for me.

Things were going well. I was getting along with my daughter-in-law, Mark was progressing in his rehab, and I was getting ready to go back to Michigan with plans to return for Mark's navy retirement party. On the day I left, as I was sitting in the cab saying my good-byes, I was surprised to see that both of them were crying. They each gave me a hug and I began to cry too, particularly touched to see Eva showing such emotion. It wasn't until I was on my way to the airport that it hit me and I started to laugh. They hadn't been crying because I was leaving. They were crying because they were attached to the puppy. But I didn't feel slighted. I'd had a good visit with them.

We made it home, after a bad trip with the puppy whining and pooping in the carry on bag. Anyone who has a Jack Russell knows how nervous and full of pep these dogs can be. Five hours in a bag had to have been miserable for him. But we did it and it was a great feeling for me to have him, although I was still missing my sweet little Maggie.

AS GOOD AS IT GETS

After that visit I called Mark and Eva every day. I loved talking with my son and I was finding it easy to speak with Eva too. He was continuing to make progress in his recovery everyday, even though he still had his arm in a cast and would have to wear it for a long time. Now that I was home I had time to think, and the whole situation made my heart ache. I still spent many hours wondering what the final outcome would be, how far he would progress, and I often wondered, *Is this as good as it gets?*

Soon it was time to go back to California for Mark's retirement party, and I thanked God for another opportunity to see how he was doing. Andy Crout-Hamel, one of his best friends in the SEALs, had arranged the celebration. I checked into a hotel and booked rooms for Jacki, Michele and her youngest son, Ryder, who would be arriving a week later. He would be the first of my grandchildren to see Mark since the accident occurred.

It was great to be back in California again and it was exciting to witness the progress that Mark had been telling me about over the phone. He could now stand by himself. His friend Foot had been helping by putting Mark on the floor and showing him how to get himself up. They did this over and over again until he was able to do it on his own. There were still things he couldn't do, as I realized when he asked me to put a blanket on him. But he was walking better, although he was still quite attached to the couch. He was talking more, and his speech was clearer. It was an effort for him to do any of the things he was doing, but he did them anyway.

The wonderful thing about Mark was that he was always in a good mood. I often thought how much more difficult this would have been if he hadn't had such a positive attitude. I wondered how he could do it. Many people had commented that, had they been in Mark's situation, they wouldn't have made it. Yet, he was always joking—sometimes to the point of excess—but you couldn't help but to laugh, even when what he said was "inappropriate", a new word he had come to learn very quickly. He had heard it from his physical therapist, his wife, his friends and from myself many times. Now, he would say something, then add, "But I guess that's inappropriate." I remember one particular occasion during the time that Bill Clinton was having all his troubles over the Monica Lewinski affair. We were watching the story unfold in the news and Mark commented, "I guess I'm not the only one who's behavior isn't appropriate," And he would laugh and laugh.

The day before the ceremony, I mentioned to Eva that Jacki would be here for the festivities. She responded by saying, "Why is she coming? She and I don't get along." I reminded her that Jacki was coming to see her brother, and that she had been there when he became a SEAL—before Eva had known Mark—and now she would be here to see him retire from the navy. I knew Eva was upset, but I made it clear that I didn't want to discuss the matter.

The next morning, Mark told me that he had had a nightmare the night before. "I dreamed that Jacki was coming," he said. I suggested that his wife had had a nightmare and he started to laugh. When I reminded him of how his sister had been there when he was down, and that she was excited to see that he was on his way to recovery, that was good enough for him, and his attitude put an end to the issue for me.

I couldn't tell Jacki a second time not to come and see her brother. It would have broken her heart. I couldn't understand how Eva could hold a grudge that long. Jacki had gotten over their previous incident and was willing to be friends with her, and had even sent her presents for her birthday.

Finally, Jacki, Michele and Ryder arrived and the day came for Mark's retirement. We followed Eva and Mark to Coronado Beach, a place where Mark and his SEAL teammates had run many times. They were already there and were cooking hot dogs and hamburgers on the grill. A tent had been set up and there were coolers full of beer; everything needed for a good picnic was in place. Many of his other friends were arriving. Foot and Bill took Mark under the arms and helped him walk through the thick sand to the tent where they would have the ceremony. When I saw all of these young men—all of them so healthy—my heart heavy again. It seemed that every time I began to feel positive about Mark's recovery, something would happen that would put it into a different perspective. I knew then that this was going to be a difficult day, one filled with both tears and joy. But Mark's good mood and happiness to see his friends was so genuine that I had to be as brave as he was.

Coronado was beautiful that day. It was warm and sunny and the vastness of the sea was a lovely background. On the wide sandy beach, there was a large open-air wooden hut with a slatted roof and a cement platform with benches and tables, where everyone was gathered, both inside and out. The SEAL team guys were dressed casually in their short khaki shorts and SEAL tee shirts. There were a few guys cooking burgers on a grill, and some of their wives had come too. We had Mark sit outside with family and friends, who were milling around while we waited for the Navy SEAL Leapfrog team to make an appearance in the sky. They were doing a jump in Mark's honor, and it wasn't long before they were overhead and descending toward us. We all cheered as they sailed through the sky in formation, with pink smoke coming from their heels for effect. The SEALs on the ground yelled, "Hoo Yah!" One of Mark's new friends, a man he'd met in the hospital, had brought his video camera to tape the event for Mark.

They landed as expected not far from our gathering, and after pulling their chutes back together, they came to talk to Mark. We then all went inside, and some stood while others sat on the benches. Mark was seated in front by himself, and the formal ceremony began.

The officer in charge called the other officers to attention and he addressed Mark with the following commendation:

This is to certify that the Secretary of the Navy has awarded the Navy and Marine Corps accommodation medal to boatswain mate second class SEAL Mark Harry Colburn, United States Navy for meritorious service. While serving as a demonstration parachutist for the Navy parachute team at Naval special warfare center from January 1996 through June 1998.

Petty Officer Colburn demonstrated outstanding professional skill and unprecedented dedication to duty while successfully executing over 100 precision parachute demonstrations in front of more than 7,000,000 spectators throughout the United States. He also managed over $120,000 in parachute equipment and supplies and implemented a new tracking system designed to monitor reserve repack cycles, insuring maintenance is properly performed in a timely manner. Petty Officer Colburn's professionalism and devotion to duty reflected great credit upon himself and were keeping with the highest tradition of the United States Naval Service.

T.R. Richards
Rear Admiral, United States Navy

Commander Naval Special Warfare Command

Then he called everyone to attention again and he read this to Mark:

Certificate of Appreciation for service in the armed forces of the United States.

Boatswain mate second class SEAL Mark Harry Colburn, United States Navy. I extend to you my personal thanks and the sincere appreciation of your nation for your honorable service. You helped to maintain the security of the United States of America with a devotion to duty that is in keeping with the proud tradition of our armed forces. I honor your service and respect life-commitment loyalty you displayed over the years. My best wishes to you for happiness and success in the future.

President Clinton

Commander in Chief

At this point Mark began to laugh and wanted to speak, and what he said was, "It's very nice of the President—with all his problems with Miss Lewinski—to do this for me." The SEALs chuckled, and I thank God that he was sort of slurring his words that day. I was hoping that nobody would understand, but I know that at least a few people heard what he said because I could tell they were trying not to laugh.

Then the last letter was read. It was from The Department of the Navy, Special Warfare Center:

From commanding officer, Naval Special Warfare Center to Mark Harry Colburn. Letter of appreciation for honorable and loyal service. On the occasion of your retirement after eight years Naval service I am proud to express on behalf of the President of the United States, the Secretary of Defense, the Secretary of the Navy, the Chief of Naval Operations and your shipmates, my sincere appreciation for the loyal service you have dedicated to your country. As you review your career you may also do so with the pride and satisfaction that stems from your professional accomplishment and performance of the duty while serving with the Naval warfare community. During your career you helped foster and preserve the strong and honorable tradition of the United States Navy. I join with all your shipmates, past and present, in wishing you every success in future endeavors. It is our sincere wish that you enjoy good health and happiness in the years ahead. I extend to you the sailors traditional benediction of fair winds and following seas, and may you enjoy the smooth sailing that you have so fully earned.

J. McGuire

They also gave Eva some flowers and a testimonial letter, telling her how they appreciated her care of her husband, Mark Colburn. Then they read a poem that I wrote for the SEALs:

They are few and they are brave
and they are strong, with nerves of steel
Our country's pride, the Navy SEALs
In peace or war, unsung heroes,
sea, air and land never stand still
Our country's pride, the Navy SEALs
One of their bros fell from the sky
night and day, they came to pray
At his side, he was so still
they gave him strength, the Navy SEALs
that bro is back, a miracle from God and love and family
My country's pride, that's how I feel
You're all my sons, the Navy SEALs

Then the SEALs got in a line and came to shake Mark's hand and say a few words to him. Looking at their faces, you could tell that they were proud of him, and they were happy that he was alive. I don't remember ever being so proud of my son—yet also so sad.

When all the navy personnel had congratulated Mark, we hugged and kissed him, and then the party started. Everybody was in a festive mood. At one point, I stood back and just observed. This was another turning point in Mark's life; his retirement from the navy. He was sitting there surrounded by his teammates and friends, smiling and joking with everyone. He was laughing and enjoying himself more than he had done in a very long time. I hoped that the video tape would turn out well so that Mark, as he progressed in his recovery, could further appreciate this special day. He loved being around people, just as he had all his life, and I thanked God that he was still the same.

I left Mark with his friends and Michele and I went and talked with a nurse who had been there when he had first opened his eyes. She hugged me, smiled and said, "See, I told you he was going to come out of it." I look back at those days now and remember how hopeless I felt then. I would never have believed that good things were ever going to happen. But now, whenever Mark wasn't doing as well as I would hope, I'd look back to those early days and realize that he was doing better than anyone could've ever expected. Still, he had a long, long way to go. Again I wondered if this would be as good as it gets, but I refused to believe that now. I knew he would get better.

The neuro-psychiatrist was at the party, as was Dr. Stone. As we were talking about how well Mark was doing, The neuro-psychiatrist told Michele and I that it was his opinion that the fact that Mark was not walking on his own might possibly be a psychological problem. He said, "He should be able to do that by now, but I believe he doesn't because he's afraid to fall. I was wondering what you'd think if I arranged to have him jump again. Michele, only half-joking, walked over to him and put her hands loosely around his neck and said, "Don't even think about it!" And I added, "Well, if that happens, I don't want to see it. You'd have to do it when I'm not around." I was really joking when I said this because I never thought it would actually take place.

The next day the girls, Ryder and I took Mark to a movie starring Jim Carrey, one of his favorite actors. Eva wanted to stay home and rest, so the four of us took off. We decided we'd walk Mark into the cinema without his wheelchair, which turned out to be quite a mistake. Although Jacki and Michele were holding Mark under the arms, it was a long walk from the parking lot to the seats of the theater. The movie had started at four o'clock and although we arrived at three thirty we missed the beginning, as it took us an hour to get to the seats, but we watched the rest of the picture. His doctor said it would be unlikely for someone with a brain injury to sit through a whole movie, but Mark's love for films was so great that it didn't bother him at all.

The following day Jacki, Michele and Ryder flew back to their homes. They felt bad about leaving Mark behind, just as I did whenever I had to leave. I'm sure they felt the same emotions that I did. When you could be with him the situation was easier to bear, but when you were away and you thought about him it was terribly hard.

The next weekend I also headed home, leaving Eva and Mark to continue their lives together. I had been there about two weeks when I got a phone call from Mark. He said to me in a weak but excited voice, "Mom, I jumped again today! The neuro-psychiatrist and I went to the same field where I crashed and he had me do a tandem jump with another jumper. The neuro-psychiatrist did a tandem jump, too, right behind me. I jumped again, I can't believe I did that! They promised me a burrito if I did the jump."

My breathing became difficult as I tried to gather my thoughts. I was stunned. Although I knew he was okay since he was on the phone telling me this, I couldn't help thinking *Who's stupid idea was it to have him jump?* The picture in my mind was of my very fragile and unsteady son (still wearing a cast on his left arm from his most recent surgery) being helped to a plane and having to jump out, tandem or not. Being told that jumping again would "help" him walk without fear was more than I could handle, and the necessary "burrito promise" just added fuel to the fire. I never in a million years imagined that The neuro-psychiatrist was serious about this "therapy" and that Eva would go along with it as well. We knew that Mark didn't walk well because of his brain injury. He was also knocked unconscious before he began to fall, so how could we know that this reenactment would have anything to do with his success at walking on his own again.

I could not let Mark know how I felt as he was telling me about this jump. He was easily influenced by other's emotions and I didn't want to upset him. I was angry and frustrated, but all I could do was tell myself to stay cool. Then Eva took the phone. "The neuro-psychiatrist jumped, too," she told me, "and he was just as scared as Mark, but Mark did real well." I asked her if he had begun to walk any differently after he jumped and she answered "no", but she thought it was good therapy for him to get over his fear. She sounded excited too, and not at all uncertain about the whole event. I had barely said goodbye and hung up when I started to cry. I called Michele right away to tell her the news. She was very upset and angry that no one had the sense to think that it might be a bad idea to take him back up to jump again, for all the obvious reasons. She believed that The neuro-psychiatrist was the one who wanted to prove something and that he orchestrated the event for his own gain. His wife and children did come to watch him; maybe she was right. Michele could not believe that anyone in their right mind would have Mark jump again, as fragile and incapable as he was to do anything on his own. She was as shaken about this as I was.

Five days or so later I got a video of the jump. It was done by a professional cameraman who filmed jumps all the time, so it was detailed and very real. There was Mark with Eva, who was holding his arm to help him walk to the airplane. In the plane, Mark was grabbing the sides of the open doorway so tightly that his fingers had to be pried open before they could get him to jump. As he was leaping, you could see nothing but fear on his face. Although Mark landed on his feet, he was still visibly shaking and pale. The neuro-psychiatrist landed on his butt, looking for all the world like Woody Allen in the movie *Sleeper*. Seeing this for the first time was horrifying to me. What on earth was the point of this?

I watched the video over and over again, thinking that the more I saw it, the more desensitized I'd be, but instead I was absolutely destroyed. Michele watched it too, and was appalled. The neuro-psychiatrist was a very religious man, and later we learned that he believed that God would take care of him and Mark during the jump. Now, I had additional concerns about how easy it was to talk Mark into doing anything when he had yet to have a will of his own. He was vulnerable and did not understand things completely. Clearly, Mark needed to be protected against people with wild ideas like this, and I was not certain that Eva was the one to do it.

There's no doubt that if it had been up to me, my son would never have jumped again. But it was not up to me, and the helplessness I felt was almost more than I could bear. I thought about everything that could've gone wrong. I thought, *What if he had had a heart attack?* The only consolation was that, when I'd asked him if he would do it again he had said, "Never! I will never jump again." I asked him if the experiment had made any difference and he said, "Heck, no."

In the end, though, God was good to my son. He protected him from everything but his own fear of falling. And it wasn't really a true fear of falling, but a fear manifested from his brain injury. I can't believe that none of the so-called professionals thought of that. I had books and folders full of explanations of brain injuries, and most people were not walking or speaking clearly. Certainly, they were not as they had been before their accidents. The only thing that would make their conditions better, besides working very hard, was time itself. The physical therapy was important, but the theme repeated over and over again was that time heals a brain, not a repetition of the circumstances that caused the injury in the first place.

Maybe in time, Mark would've had the desire to jump again, but at this time and under these circumstances he didn't ask to do it. He was coaxed into doing it by others. Sometimes I felt so overwhelmed that I wanted to roll up into a ball and just forget about everything, but I knew I had to be there. I had to see what was going to happen. It was like every other critical juncture for him; I was obsessed with seeing him return, step by step, to the person he once was.

As Mark became more coherent, he began to ask what had happened to him and if the accident had been his fault. He had no recollection of that day and had to depend on different accounts of it by his buddies. When The neuro-psychiatrist had asked him about it, Mark said that he thought that the man who tore his parachute was a giant, which prompted The neuro-psychiatrist to conclude that it was time for Mark to face the person who collided with him. The young man had come to see Mark a couple of times at the rehab center, but it was before Mark was aware of his surroundings. After Mark began to come around, he had stopped coming. I guess he didn't want to face him.

The neuro-psychiatrist arranged the meeting in his office. Mark was surprised when he saw that he was not a giant, but a SEAL just like him, someone, in fact, whom he had known. They shook hands and Mark told him that he was not angry, that he knew it was an accident. They both cried. After that, we never saw or heard from that young man again. Mark still hears from the other SEALs every now and then, but not hearing from this person still hurts him.

JUMPING AGAIN

Mark's friends would often stop by and take him to the cinema. He would call and tell me that Foot had come to take him out to eat and then go to the movies, or how Scott Benjamin, Mark's friend and lawyer, had done the same. He also had visits from Mark Flemming, whom he'd known from the days when they worked at Ford Motor Company and shared an apartment. Mark Flemming had paid for a yearlong membership at a local gym for Mark and would take him there to exercise. Eva took him there, too, and the people at the gym would help him work out. All this time he was still going to physical therapy as well.

Mark was anxious to begin classes at The Brain School, which had been recommended jointly by Drs. Farrow and Stone. The only thing he needed to be able to do before starting was to walk with the aid of a walker. In time he was ready. Eva would take him there in the morning, and then he'd be dropped off in the afternoon by the school's shuttle. He called me after his classes started and told me how much he loved going to school again, but that it took him a long time to get around inside the building, as he was very slow with his walker.

Late one night I got a call from Eva and she was crying. She said that she had had an argument with Mark and that he was throwing videos all over the place. I asked her what the argument was about and she said that Mark just got mad out of the clear-blue sky. But when I spoke with him, he told me that Eva said that he couldn't walk anywhere without help. At that time, he was trying to use a walker, but his arms were weak and his legs weren't much stronger. It seems that he wanted a video that Eva wouldn't give him, and when he got angry, she dared him to walk and get it himself. They were both hysterical so it was hard to know exactly what was going on between the two of them. He also told me that he broke a vase that her brother had given them as a wedding present. I tried to calm him down, but I could tell that he was very agitated. Afterward, Eva called The neuro-psychiatrist who prescribed some Tegretol. When I heard about this I was disturbed, because Mark was usually in such a good mood and I worried about the effects of this drug.

Shortly after this had happened, I had to fly down to Florida for a funeral. Nicholas's grandmother had died of Lou Gehrig's disease and both Jacki and

Nicholas were very close to her. When I got back I talked with Eva and told her where I'd been and why I went. I made the mistake of telling her that I felt sorry for Jacki because she loved her son's grandmother and was very sad to lose her. I'd forgotten how angry Eva could get, Especially when it came to Jacki. She began to tell me how she disliked her, seemingly forgetting that she was talking about my daughter. Her timing couldn't have been worse and I lost my temper, even though I had promised myself that I wouldn't do that again. I told her that she had no reason to be the way she was with Jacki, and that she was trying to turn Mark against her, as well. I told her that Jacki was Mark's sister and that nothing she would tell him could ever change that, and that he would always love her.

I believe she hung up on me. I called back and talked to Mark and told him that I'd gotten angry with Eva and that I was sorry. But since his accident, no one could talk to him about anything that was controversial because he didn't like to hear any of it. After that, every time I called, Eva would quickly say, "I'll let you talk to Mark." As it turned out, I would never be close to her again.

In the summer, Eva agreed to let Mark come back to Michigan and spend a couple of weeks with us while she went to Santa Barbara for her girlfriend's wedding. That was fine with us and it was great to have Mark home again. One day I took him to Mackinac Island, a quaint place that is free of automobiles and is steeped in history. We boarded the ferry, with Mark in his wheelchair, and headed over to the island to have a picnic. There we sat on the grass and strolled by the storefronts before taking the ferry back to the mainland and driving back to Petoskey. I remember having no difficulty with putting his wheelchair in the trunk. I realized that I was so strong since the time he'd had his accident and that I never at any time felt any pain, which was odd because I have arthritis. I also had a hunch that sooner or later it would catch up with me, though, it hadn't yet. As long as I was with Mark, I felt strong and invigorated.

The two weeks passed swiftly and soon it was time for Mark to return to California. We had had a good time with him and it was difficult to have him leave again, but I was thankful for the chance for him to be home. Michele and I drove him to Detroit and he flew from Metro Airport back to San Diego.

Mark continued to tell us how much he liked his new school and his teachers. Things seemed to be all right between him and Eva again, but she was so strange with me over the phone. I could feel the cold through the line. I'd try to make conversation, but it was to no avail. I sent presents to them for every possible occasion, but nothing seemed to work. Since I knew that when I was home I couldn't help but call them every day, I finally decided to put some space between us.

As it happened, my niece, Daniele, in France, was going through some troublesome times of her own just then. Her daughter had been experiencing a difficult pregnancy. She'd been in the hospital for three months, and when the baby was born, two months prematurely, the child had to be kept in an incubator. My niece had worried terribly for her daughter's life. With all that was happening with Mark, I hadn't been able to be with her and I felt bad about that. I loved Daniele and had always felt close to her. Now, when she invited me to come to France to see the baby, and her son's wife, who was about to have a baby, too, I thought it would be a good time for me to go. I called Eva and Mark and told them that I'd be going to France for eight days and that I'd call them as often as I could from there. I didn't get a response one way or another from Eva.

The events of the past eight months had been overwhelming, but I tried my best to put it aside for a little while, and I boarded my plane and flew to Paris. It was good to see Daniele and her husband again. Daniele is a successful director/screen writer in France. We went to St. Tropez where her father had a house, and she absolutely spoiled me. She had made some wonderful movies and I had the good fortune of being able to see several of them.

I called Mark once while I was there. Of course I got the same cool reception from Eva as she quickly gave the phone to Mark. As I spoke with him, I noticed that his voice sounded different, perhaps a bit low. I found myself missing him again. I had a very nice, relaxing time in France, and after spending a week with my niece and her two new arrivals, it was time for me to go home.

When I got back to Michigan, I called Mark, who sounded so exhausted that I could hardly hear him. I asked him if he was okay, but he was slurring his words and I could hardly understand him. I spoke with Eva and asked her the same question. She told me that he was all right, but tired. I called the next day and Mark sounded the same, his voice so low again that I could scarcely hear him. I asked him if he was depressed and he said that he was a little bit. Once again, I spoke to Eva and asked her if Mark was depressed, to which she tersely replied, "Of course he's depressed. You'd be depressed too if you couldn't walk or swallow and had all the problems that he has." She continued with a litany of everything that Mark couldn't do. I sensed that the best thing I could do was drop the subject with her.

The next day I called The neuro-psychiatrist and told him my fears, and asked him not to mention my call to Eva because she'd think that I was implying that Mark's depression was her fault—which I wasn't. The neuro-psychiatrist told me that he'd actually heard the same thing from the school. My heart sank. I called Mark again and asked if he wanted me to come and he said no, that it would make things worse. That made me really worry.

During this time, Michele continued to have a decent relationship with Eva. She talked to her often and tried to keep up with how things were going for both of them. Eva seemed to confide in her and Michele struggled to keep the peace between all of us. The phone conversations about the difficulties she and Mark were facing became more frequent. It became obvious to Michele that both Mark and Eva were unhappy and depressed. Eva expressed interest in going back to UCSD to finish her Art History degree and Michele encouraged her to do it, telling her that we would take care of Mark so she could finish school. It seemed to be a good solution for all of us, and Michele thought it offered Eva an opportunity for a much needed break from life as Mark's caregiver. When she called to tell me that Eva would be bringing Mark to Michigan for three months, I could hardly believe my ears. My heart was filled with joy.

I was so happy and I began to prepare the house, getting it ready for my son. Michele said that both Eva and Mark would come for Christmas and stay through New Year's. Then Eva would go back and begin her classes. I really didn't care what she was going to do anymore. All I could think of was that I'd have Mark here with me. Still, I was surprised that Eva was leaving him here because she was still angry with me.

They arrived four days before Christmas. I welcomed them both. It was good to see Mark, and I tried to be as nice as I could to Eva. I was so thankful to have him for three full months. But soon my joy was replaced by concern as I witnessed them interact with one another. It started on the first evening they were at my home. I had put Eva and Mark in the upstairs guest room, and when Mark went to bed, Eva sat on the couch and watched TV. Soon after, Mark woke up and asked me to help him down the stairs. When we got to the living room, Eva got up and went upstairs immediately. Then, when he asked to go back up, she came down as soon as he returned to the room. It was obvious that she didn't want to be next to him, but he didn't seem to realize that she was pushing him away.

I had told Eva that she could use my car whenever she wanted to, so the next day she asked to borrow it to go to a little Indian store that Mark had loved because the owners had a dog that was part wolf. Mark loved to play with it. When Eva said that she was going there, Mark asked if he could go, too, but she stomped her foot in disgust and said, "Well, if you're going to go then I'm not." I said, "Eva, why don't you take him? He loves to play with the dog they have there." Finally she agreed, but within fifteen minutes they were back and she was wearing that scowling face again.

Another time I was coming down the stairs and she was in the den, trying to fix the wrap on Mark's hand that kept his fingers straight. I guess he wasn't holding his hand the way she wanted him to and I heard her say, "Why don't you ask your mother to do it? She loves you so much!"

I was determined not to respond. She was a guest in my house and I wasn't going to create any more aggravation for any of us. She wore an expression of angst whenever she was doing anything for Mark. And when she showed me what had to be done for him, she was very impatient. It hurt me to see that these things were such a chore for her, and he wasn't in a very good mood either. Of course, he still spoke out impulsively, but there was one thing in particular that he said that caught my attention. He would often repeat, "Well, we never make love anyway." Obviously, not having sex was something that was on his mind. This was an area where I definitely felt that it wasn't my place to say anything, but I felt my son's pain.

On the day of Christmas Eve we were sitting in the den, and as we were talking, Eva looked at Mark and said, "I think you need to shave." Mark had very little hair and he shaved perhaps once a month. He was just like his father that way; he had no hair on his chest and very little facial growth. Anyway, he looked at her defiantly and said, "I'm not going to shave until I have sex." She said, "Then you'll have a very long beard because I'm not going to have sex with you." I was rather shocked, but she looked to me and said, "And don't look so surprised."

Their sparring continued. Mark said, "Well that's nothing new. If I'm not going to have sex, then I'm not going to shave." She retorted by saying, "You're not a man, and I'll have sex when you're a man." With that I was even more shocked, and as I looked at her, she said, "Nobody understands me! Nobody understands me!" I said to her, "Yes Eva, I understand you." And I did understand her. Mark was very hard to take care of. This was a man who needed to be put in a bathtub, he needed help wherever he walked, he couldn't dress himself, he needed his food specially prepared, his wheelchair had to be hoisted in and out of the car all the time, and his drinks had to be mixed with a thickener because he couldn't swallow. There was a lot to do to take proper care of him. He was coughing a lot because he couldn't breathe as well as before, and his hand needed re-wrapping all the time. So when I said, "I do understand what you're going through," I really did.

I wanted to tell her that I wasn't a stranger to tragedy and pain, having lost my husband at a young age, and that I knew what she was going through. I said, "I lost my husband when I was forty. I know how hard things can get." She looked at Mark and then, quite deliberately said, "A death would be easier than this!"

I got up out of my chair. I wanted to throw her out onto the street. I'm sure Mark could tell how angry I was. He said, "Please...I don't want you two to argue."

I swallowed my anger, got up and put on my shoes, determined not to let the situation totally explode. I said, "Listen, Eva, I know you're taking very good care of Mark, so let's forget about this and just try to relax and enjoy this time we all have together." But I knew my words didn't really reach her, and when I touched her shoulder she pulled away as though she'd been touched by a snake. I felt so bad for Mark that I was sick. Later that night I went out and sat in the car where nobody could hear me and I cried.

Since it was Christmas Eve, I asked them if they wanted to go to midnight mass. Eva said that she was too tired, so I prepared a nice dinner, complete with candles. As we ate Mark mentioned something about being a SEAL and Eva became angry with him again and said, "You know you're not a SEAL anymore!" Things got quiet. Then Mark said, "You know you're not coming back to get me." Eva didn't answer.

That night when Eva had gone to bed, Mark was sitting by himself on the sofa, so I asked him if he wanted to go to midnight mass with me. He said no, but he asked me if we could talk. I sat down next to him and he said, "I can't live with her. I don't want to live with her anymore." I asked him if he was sure and he said, "Yes. I don't want to be with her ever again. I want to get a divorce."

I wanted to be sure that he knew what he was saying. I wanted to find out if he was saying this out of momentary anger or if he really meant it. He told me that he was sure, and he began to tell me about all the things that were bothering him. He said, "I can't live like this. I feel like I'm a burden and I don't want to be a burden to anyone and I'm made to believe that I am all the time. I don't want things to be like this anymore...I want a divorce." I couldn't believe it. We talked well into the night. I told him that I'd try to talk to Eva and tell her how he felt.

The next morning she was upstairs reading in bed. I went up to her and said, "Eva, do you know that you and Mark have a problem? He doesn't want to stay with you, and I don't want you to come back in three months and say that it's our fault that he feels that way, because he feels that way now." She looked at me with expressionless eyes and said, "I don't know anything about that. Anyway, I've decided to leave tomorrow. I have a lot of things to do before I start school and I don't want to hang around here for another week." I asked her how she felt about Mark and she said, "Well, we're not going to have any children, because if we did I'd have to take care of them and him, too, and I'm thirty-eight and I want to have a life."

Later on I overheard her telling Michele, "I think your mother has delusions about Mark's condition. This is as good as he's ever going to get." Michele countered and said, "No she doesn't. She knows very well that there's always hope."

So on the day after Christmas, Eva asked me to take her to the airport in Traverse City, which is about sixty-five miles from Petoskey. It was snowing and Michele wouldn't let me do it, offering to take Eva herself. She knew that I was upset and that it wouldn't be a good idea for me to drive, particularly given the weather conditions.

As they were getting ready to leave, Eva said her good-bye to Mark. She told him that she would call and that she'd see him soon. I was crying as I watched them. When she got in Michele's car, I thought Mark would be destroyed. But before Eva even closed the door, Mark thrust his arm into the air and said, "Good riddance! I don't want to ever see this woman again…ever, ever again! I feel so relieved that she's gone." For the first time since the accident, he was speaking in a pretty clear, understandable voice. Eva couldn't hear him, but Mark kept repeating, Goodbye and good riddance. I've never felt so relieved," as she and Michele drove away.

We went back in the house, sat down and talked more about the things that had been revealed over the past few days. I told Mark, "This would be a good place for you. It's a small town, and I promise that you'll get well here and that we'll give you all the help that we can. Your family and I will help you recover as completely as you possibly can. This isn't as good as it gets. You'll get better and better and better. I promise you that as long as I live you're going to keep getting better." He looked at me and said, "I know, Ma, and I know I will." And that was the last we saw of Eva.

THE ENCINO MAN

Mark began the next phase of his life in Petoskey, Michigan. I had set up a room for him upstairs and tried to make him as comfortable as possible. He'd brought a laptop computer with him. Since he had never used it before and I knew nothing about computers, we couldn't figure out how to operate it. I had Michele try, but she couldn't get it to work either. We sent it back to the manufacturer a couple of times, but it still didn't function properly. Finally, she said, "Why don't we just buy him a new computer?" So we purchased a desktop computer from someone she knew, a man who promised to come and service it if we had any trouble. I didn't think I could learn to use a computer at my age, but I was willing to try, or perhaps take a class or two.

Michele began to organize Mark's life. There were certain organic foods that he'd grown fond of, and I became a regular customer at the local health food store. He was also drinking a Myoplex supplement, which some of the SEALs used for energy, and I'd mix him a shake of it every morning. He still needed a lot of care, particularly since he wasn't sleeping very well at night. He would perspire terribly, to the point where I'd have to change his sheets twice during the night. Then he'd have to take a bath because he was so wringing wet. I'd help him into the tub, in which I had rails installed to make it easier for him, and then I'd help him get out and back into bed. Once as I was trying to help him upstairs he got stuck in the stairway. We began to laugh and it seemed that there was nothing we could do to get back in position to move again. He still insisted on sleeping in the bed upstairs, so I pushed and pushed him from behind. We were laughing the whole time; it can be very difficult for someone with a brain injury to do two things at once. So the whole time that he laughed, he was unable to even try to make it up the stairs. After over an hour of laughing and pushing, we finally made it.

There was a gym in town where my daughter worked out, and we went there and got a membership for Mark. When he first came in, the owners were very friendly and wanted to help him as much as possible, as they were aware of his situation. In fact, they told Michele and Mark that he could come in anytime he wanted and that he didn't have to pay. They even dedicated a portion of the gym's wall to him—posting pictures and articles—and they titled it: A LOCAL HERO. It was so nice of them and I was thankful for their kindness. Everybody he met at the gym would encourage him when the workout got tough for him.

The gym owners had called the local newspapers and, as a result, reporters came down to do a feature on Mark and his ongoing recovery. It was good publicity for them, and Mark, being the ham that he is, was more than happy to oblige. In one of the articles, someone wrote that Mark was once a Navy SEAL who was afraid of nothing, and now he was afraid to walk down his own driveway. As I was reading this, I thought, *My son is not afraid. He can't walk for other reasons, but he is not afraid.* So as we were sitting together one day I asked him, "Mark, how do you feel when you walk? Are you afraid, or do you feel dizzy?" I told him of a time when I had a bad ear infection and how it affected my balance. I explained what the feeling was like and asked him if that was the way he felt. He said, "Yes, it's something like that. It's not that I'm afraid to walk, it's that I get dizzy and that makes me hesitant." Now it made more sense to me, and I could empathize with how he was feeling. I talked to Michele and told her of our conversation. She agreed with my assessment and said that it was a lack of balance that kept him from walking, and we decided that we'd send him back to physical therapy.

We took him to meet Tim Bondy, the owner of a physical therapy center. At our first appointment we were introduced to Adam Tsaloff, whom Tim had assigned to work with Mark. That visit was wonderful because, after they did a thorough assessment, they outlined a plan that would help him. I was filled with hope that things would get better. Soon, Adam realized that Mark had an eye for good-looking girls, so he assigned Linda to work with him. She was attractive, but was also knowledgeable and she had a good sense of humor. They soon referred to themselves as the Mark and Linda show. Working together, the whole team helped Mark immensely. They took his case seriously and were so fond of my son right from the start that it was a pleasure to go there. The mood was light and the encouragement was terrific. They began by having Mark take as many steps as he could while they timed him with a stopwatch. Then the next time he came they made him take one additional step and they timed him again. It was a very slow process, but they kept doing this each time he came in. And so began another long phase in his rehabilitation.

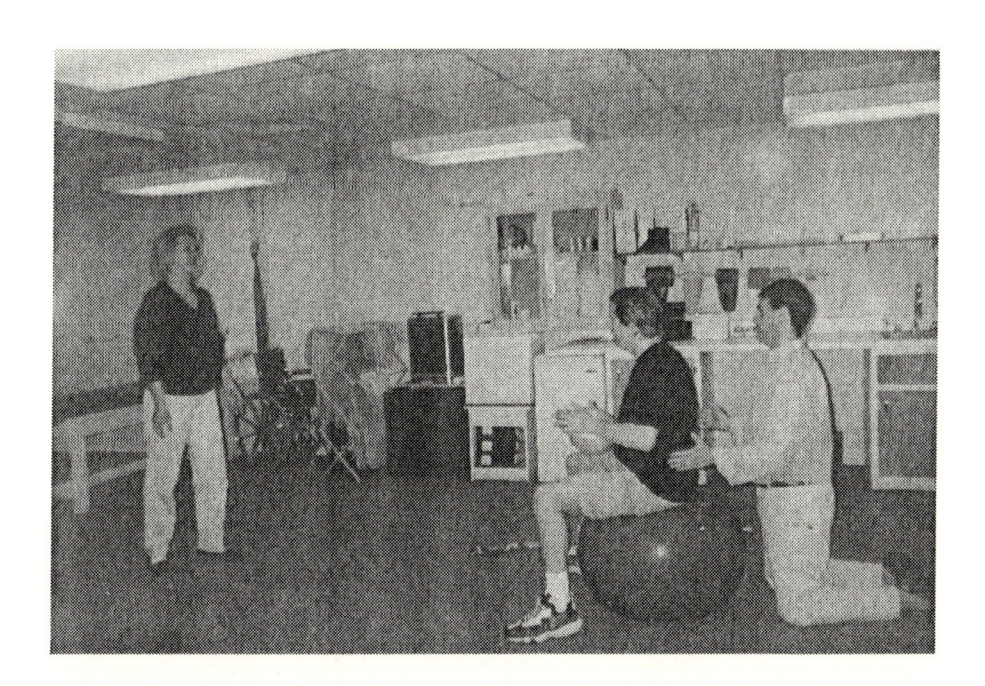

Mark's balance was so poor that, when he stood, he would sway from one side to the other. It seemed like such an impossible weakness to overcome, but each time we went to rehab he'd do a little more—from one step, to two steps, to three steps, and finally all the way down the hallway. Every time he made progress, the therapists would clap their hands in acknowledgment. His attitude was wonderful and the attitude of the people at the center was just as positive. Mark was always joking and they would joke right along with him. From the first day on, I went with him and watched everything. The other physical therapists that worked at the center were just as enthusiastic as the ones who were helping Mark. A therapist named Todd became a good friend and would often ask Mark to go to the movies with him. They were all so friendly to Mark that they became his second family.

There were still unresolved issues between Mark and Eva. When I had first told her that Mark was angry and had warned her that he wanted a divorce, she had also told me that she was only thirty-eight years old and that she had to live her life, too. So I wrote her a letter after Mark had gotten settled in with me. In it, I told her that it would be better if she let Mark go, seeing how hard it was for her to take care of him. Shortly after, she called Mark and told him about the letter, but he was so angry with her that he only reiterated that he wanted a divorce. He was calling her names and cursing, and whenever she called after that I had to remind him not to be so offensive. Every time she called, they would argue, and each time Mark would be more vulgar until she finally quit calling. There was no doubt that those exchanges affected him. He was angry a lot more. I wondered if this anger he had toward her was a phase, and every once in a while I'd ask him if he was sure that he wanted to get his divorce, but his responses were unwavering.

Finally, we called his friend Scott, the lawyer, but he said he couldn't get involved because Eva had previously been a client of his—albeit jointly with Mark—when they had lost the twins, and he recommended somebody else in the San Diego area. Michele called the attorney, then had her talk to Mark. She agreed to take care of the divorce in the most expedient and simplest way possible. We sent her firm a retainer fee immediately and all they had to do was get in touch with Eva—who knew very well that this was coming and had, in fact, asked Mark to file because she didn't want to pay for it. Directly afterward, he became so cheerful again that you could sense his relief.

One of my first jobs was to help Mark regain his confidence. I kept reminding him that he was going to get better, and that when he improved, it was still not the end of the road, but he'd get even better from that point. I told him that he had my unwavering support, and the support of his sisters and extended family, as well.

I knew that he missed his apartment by the sea. He had chosen it himself and he loved being near the ocean. He told me that, even if he had to walk there, his goal was to see the ocean again. I promised him that in a little while we'd take a trip to California so that he could see the place where he used to swim and surf. He was dying to go back into the green room—the green room of the ocean that was his escape from the real world.

Getting his confidence back proved to be easy. Mark was a very determined, positive and strong person and those traits were useful to him now, as was his training as a Navy SEAL. I knew that if he were given half a chance, he would do the rest. Even with all the struggles ahead and the challenges of everyday life, he was never going to give up, which made it all the easier for those working with him, and for myself, too. I drew strength from him, as well. I made up my mind that I would never cry in front of him or be negative in any way. I would only show him all the good that was waiting for him.

Mark had learned a lot about brain injuries from the school he had attended in California, but the only thing I didn't care for was the lack of positive reinforcement as far as setting goals was concerned. The doctors there stressed that no one should expect too much, and that they should accept that there'd be things that they would never be able to do again. Mark would sometimes say, even though he was only paraphrasing, that he was told that he was only half the man he used to be. I looked him in the eye and told him, "Mark, you're going to be a different man. You're going to be your own hero—and that's what you should aim for." Michele was there for him, too. Every time I wanted to do something new for him, I only had to ask her and she'd put me in touch with whomever I needed to talk with, find out what we had to do, where we had to go to keep him learning and moving forward in his recovery.

Since I want to help others who are in the same situation as my son, I should describe in detail where Mark was, at this point of his recovery. First of all, he couldn't walk more than three or four steps by himself. After that he either needed to be supported or he held onto someone's shoulder. He needed help talking his baths and getting dressed, but he was doing more and more by himself all the time. Since he lacked that imaginary filter between the brain and the tongue, he would still speak out impulsively, always telling the truth, no matter how bitter that might be. But he was always in a good mood. He was as sweet a man as possible, except when he spoke to Eva. He'd get up in the morning and say, "Good morning. Did you sleep well?" He would always say thank you whenever anyone did something for him. All and all, it was pleasant to have him around.

Mark and I had a wonderful rapport. We shared a lot of laughs, watched the same television shows and did the same silly things. I was more than used to doing these silly little things with my children when they were young, and later with my grandchildren. Any time we did these things I was a child with them, like laughing at and telling corny jokes. But underneath all that, Mark knew that I was strong and that I'd be there for him.

Mark would sleep with his door open at night, and I'd keep mine open as well. Given the way he was breathing I was always afraid that he would choke, so I slept light in those days. He was taking a mild sedative at night and an antidepressant during the day. He'd put on a lot of weight and most of his pants had to have elastic around the waist because he was gaining weight so quickly. Finally, Michele and I decided that it was time for him to lose a few pounds, so we put him on a diet of vegetables, chicken, and Myoplex mixed with milk. He drank a lot of juice, still mixed with thickener, although it was difficult to find one that tasted good mixed that way. Once in a while he'd crave Coca Cola, even though he didn't usually care for it, and he wanted to have water without the thickener, but he couldn't have that either.

His physical therapy was reduced from three visits a week to twice weekly. He was still going to the gym as well. He also started seeing a neuro-feedback specialist who said that she could help him walk, Mark objected to it at first because it was very expensive. He wanted someone who could get him to walk again through hypnosis, and when he found out that she couldn't do that, he lost faith. Still, he was getting a massage once a week and also doing some yoga. It was time for him to give up his wheelchair, too. He had a very good walker with wheels and a basket on the front that he used instead.

Whenever Mark went to physical therapy or to the gym he'd come home, lay on the couch and sleep for two to three hours. When he did this, he would ask me to take the blanket from the foot of the couch and put it on him, since doing it himself involved a motion that he still found difficult. He had trouble taking charge of things, too. He loved movies, though, and it was good to see that he was able to watch one from beginning to end without losing interest. He had difficulty reading so I got him some books on tape, and whenever we'd travel in the car he'd listen to them. I never watched a TV show unless it was one that Mark liked, and if he was watching something, I would watch it too.

It wasn't long before Mark began to use his walker more. Getting up to the bedroom wasn't so difficult anymore, but making his way down the stairs in the morning was more of a problem. Sometimes he found it easier to walk down backwards. He worked on that movement in the gym, too. He also rode a stationary bike and was in a spinning class. On several occasions the Navy SEAL in him came out and he would pedal quite fast, and begin screaming at the fifteen others who were riding stationary bikes, "Quit now! Quit now! Avoid the rush!" just like they did during hell-week in the SEAL initiation stage. His sister did one of the classes with him, and after seeing what he was doing, let him know that it wasn't a good thing to yell at the class. Since I didn't go to the gym I didn't realize what was going on. Finally, the instructor felt that Mark was disrupting the class, so we had him drop it. One good thing about the bike riding, though, was that he'd lost his excess weight and all his pants fit again.

That first year, whenever Mark walked by himself he looked a little like Frankenstein, with his arms straight out; obviously, the earth seeming such an uncertain place to him. What was amazing, though, was that no matter how much he was hurting or how he felt, he never, ever complained. His good humor rubbed off on all of us. I remember his sister commenting that she couldn't complain about anything, seeing that Mark didn't, despite all he'd been through. I came to realize that if he ever did tell me that something was wrong or hurting, I would take it very seriously and knew that it must really be bothering him.

It was so hard for him to do the things he was doing. A brain injury is something that overwhelms you with fatigue. But you could never stop him. He just kept on going and going. In fact, he used to call himself the Energizer Eveready Battery. Sometimes his physical efforts were successful, while other times he would see no results. The same applied to his mental endeavors.

His sister called the community college and found a woman who helped students with special needs. At first she wasn't sure Mark was ready. This was when he could hardly walk, and, as she observed, it looked like he was holding the walls whenever he tried. But he had that great personality and sense of charm and she finally agreed that he could attend. We asked Mark what he would like to take and he said drama. I wanted to say, *How can you take drama? You can hardly speak,"* but I didn't have the heart to tell him that. And it was a good thing, too, because I was in for a big surprise.

Mark's first teacher's name was Greg Baird, and I'll never forget him because he was one of the most patient and understanding men that I'd ever met. I explained Mark's situation, but he was already familiar with Mark's condition because of all the newspaper and television stories. I'd drive Mark to the college and help him get to his class, with him hanging onto my shoulder as we walked down the hall. Once he was in class I'd go home, then return three hours later to get him. All the time I'd wonder what was happening. As for Greg Baird, he became a good friend. He was one of those rare, wonderful people who would do whatever it took to help somebody. He coached Mark with his lines and saw to it that he fit in with the class. He had to put up with a lot because Mark would still speak impulsively, and whenever somebody spoke he had to put his two cents in. Most of the time it was funny, but sometimes it was not funny at all. Still, it was the type of class where everybody would understand. So Greg would tell Mark to keep quiet when he had to, which was exactly what Mark needed.

One day Greg took me aside after I dropped my son off and told me that Mark had done something out of line. He explained that, during a dress rehearsal, somebody had put makeup on Mark which made him look as though blood were running down his face. Apparently he had gone to the class in session next door, walked in and announced, "I'm hurt!" before collapsing on the floor. Thinking he was really hurt, the teacher bent down to look at him, whereupon Mark said, "Why don't you kiss me?" Because, understandably enough, the woman was pretty upset, I had Mark take her some flowers the next day. And I told him that he was never to interrupt another class again. I was afraid that someone would say that he couldn't attend classes anymore, but Greg stuck with him, and I believe he even gave him a B for the semester. So Mark began his college life.

He had also taken a computer class, and I did too, but it was so complicated that neither of us got much out of it. I ended up buying the book, *Computers for Dummies*. Michele would come over and help us with it, too, and finally we were able to get online on our own. From that point on, Mark took to it quickly. I tried my best, and after a while I got the hang of it, too. It was a personal triumph for me since I had never thought I'd be able to operate a computer. The first thing that Mark did was go into a chat room for people with brain injuries, and it became his home away from home. Everyone in the room had a nickname—Mark was Underfrog—and they talked to each other, comparing notes on their injuries. Sometimes the people were funny, sometimes they were depressed, and sometimes they just talked about day-to-day things.

Trying to navigate our way around the internet was the only thing that made Mark and I argue. He would tell me how to do something and I'd say that it wasn't that way, or vice-versa, and we'd fight back and forth for a while, but then we'd both end up laughing. Finally, he met a girl online whose mother was a computer expert and she helped us a lot. It was nice because we didn't have to rely so much on Michele.

Mark was able to write his story, like all the others at the brain-injury site. It was at www.tbichat.org. It was a great site for Mark and soon he became friendly with everyone there. They had a place where you could post photos and he placed some of them on that site.

He was still in a world of his own, with poor short-term memory, not knowing which day it was, and asking the same questions over and over again. The internet opened a door to the rest of the world, and through that, Mark found romance. After he wrote his story on the TBI website, he received an e-mail and pictures from a young, beautiful girl with pale white skin and long black hair. Her name was Melody. She seemed to know her way around the computer quite well. Many times I had to help Mark get online to answer her, because he wouldn't remember how to do it from the day before because of his short-term memory problem. Still, he was excited about this new world and he immersed himself into it. He could only type with one finger because of the injury to his left hand; ultimately, however, he could type faster with that one finger than some people could with both hands.

His correspondence with his beautiful new friend soon began to consume most of his days. She sent some risqué e-mail photos of her in her underwear. The next time they conversed, she told Mark that she used to be a beauty queen and that she was twenty-two years old. She continued to send photos and every picture she sent was beautiful. She and Mark "chatted" every day, and then one night they decided to talk to each other on the phone. I dialed the number that she had sent and handed the phone to Mark. Unfortunately, it was very difficult to understand her and Mark could only make out a few words. I realized that her brain injury was even more serious than my son's. Her mother took the phone and told Mark what she said. It was so much different than their chat room conversations. She gave short, simple answers, and it took a long time to answer questions. I guessed that using the computer was much easier for her than talking.

Melody and Mark continued to talk online, and soon a romance blossomed. They began to talk on the phone every night with Melody's mother as the interpreter. They called each other pet names and sent presents through the mail.

Finally, after about six months, they decided that they were going to meet. Realizing that my son needed romance in his life, I made plans to take him to Melody's house in Florida.

Eva had left Mark with the impression that sex was something that he wasn't going to have anymore, which hurt his pride but not his will. To know that a girl was interested in my son was important to me, as well, because even more than sex, he needed the excitement that this scenario brought to him. Before meeting Melody, Mark had gone to Florida for a reunion with his friend, Bill. When he returned, he told me, "If Eva were here I could tell her that I shaved in Florida." I didn't ask any questions, but I was glad to know that he had proved to himself that he was a man in every respect.

Having a relationship with this girl was very self-affirming for Mark. Being in love, writing her poems, and talking to her every night on the phone was great, even though her mother still had to tell Mark what she was saying. Finally, I told Mark to tell her mother that he wanted to talk directly to Melody, even if he couldn't understand everything she said.

Mark was very eager to see her, and I was excited for him. I had talked to her mother, Adele, several times, and we both were looking forward to our kids getting together and sharing a little happiness after all the misery they had both gone through. Adele told me that Melody's brain injury had been caused by a terrible car accident. I didn't know how things were going to turn out, but I was amazed by Melody's beauty in the pictures her mother would send. However, I must confess that I was also somewhat surprised that her mother was so eager to send pictures of her daughter wearing Victoria's Secret type negligees.

When we arrived in Florida, they were waiting for us at the airport; a tall, dark-haired, pleasant looking woman with a girl who looked like a doll. Immediately, Mark took Melody in his arms. They looked like such a beautiful couple together, but when Mark took a few steps with his arm around her, it was clear that she had a difficult time walking on her own. As we drove to their house, Melody and Mark sat in the back while her mother and I talked about our children's accidents and compared stories. It was obvious to me that Melody had a lot further to go in her recovery than Mark did. She had those all-to-familiar moments where she would drift off with a vacant look on her face and leave us. When we talked to her she would answer, but she had difficulty speaking.

Melody's house was set up to accommodate her well. She had a gym and a hot tub in one room, and a piano and her computer in another. It was a lovely house. Mark and I had arranged to stay in a nearby hotel, since we really had not met them until now. After the first night, Adele thought that the four of us should get a suite by the ocean and enjoy the next few days on the beach.

Mark was very happy and he didn't seem to mind that Melody was not very talkative. While her mother and I chatted in the hotel room, Mark and Melody would gently kiss. Before I left home, I had told Mark to go easy and not to try anything with Melody. I was concerned about him being too aggressive, along with the fact that he would probably still say whatever was on his mind without thinking of the consequences. I continued to remind him to be respectful and not to embarrass her or me. When I saw them together, I knew that he would comply with my wishes.

Adele was devoted to her daughter, but there was something to their relationship that seemed different. I concluded that before her daughter's accident, Adele had been a "stage" mom, helping her daughter to become a beauty queen. It seemed that she continued to be determined to fulfill her daughter's dreams, and hers, to the limits of possibility. Melody was still beautiful with her long, wavy-brown hair and her delicate, thin body. I realized that Adele was in control of every aspect of her daughter's life. As it was, she would give Melody her shower, put on her makeup, pick out her clothes, and dress her in ways that made her look like a model. I asked her if she did this everyday and she said, "Yes, I do all this and her nails, too. I try to keep her just the way she was before the accident." It was sad to watch, yet I recognized myself in Adele in many ways. I learned a lot about myself from the experience of watching another mother reacting to the tragedy of her child's brain injury.

On the second night Mark asked me if he could sleep in the same bed as Melody. I told him he could not, but her mother said that it would be all right and that she would sleep with them. As shocked as I was, I agreed, and Mark went into their room. I was surprised to hear Melody's mother tell me that she had brought some protection. I'm sure I gave her quite the puzzled look, and she said, "Well you never know if they're going to do anything." I thought it was strange for a mother to do such a thing, especially under these circumstances. I told her that I didn't think it would be proper for our two kids to engage in sex at this point. She asked me if Mark had had sex since the accident. I told her that he had been married and that I assumed that he had, but I was rather uncomfortable talking about this with her.

In the morning I asked Mark how everything had gone and he said, "Don't worry, Mom. Nothing happened. I took my Trazadone and it put me to sleep right away."

The whole situation was like everything else in his life, completely unconventional and dreamlike. I often thought that if someone were to read everything that we'd gone through, they wouldn't believe it. But that's the way life with Mark was, intense and strange and amazing. Sometimes I would think, *What in the world am I doing here? How can this be happening?*

Overall, our visit was pleasant and the Jones' hospitality was wonderful. But when we got home, the e-mails Mark received from Melody were even more intense and I became somewhat worried about where this would go. He continued to send her presents and it seemed to make his life a little sweeter. Eventually, the e-mails became less frequent, and the content not as romantic as it had been. This became a source of frustration for Mark and often he would become angry. One day while in the chat room, Melody wrote that she thought they had become too close, and that she should be spending more time with her friends. As they chatted about this, Mark called me to the computer screen and pointed out how fast Melody's replies were coming. "She isn't typing this—her mother is!" he told me, and I agreed.

Direct as always, Mark wrote back and told Melody what he thought was happening. She denied it, but I realized that he was right and that for the past eight months he had been, in essence, in a relationship with Melody's mother. As I paid closer attention to what was being written, I noticed that a lot of it was of a more mature nature than what any twenty-two year old would say. Adele was not only dressing her up like a doll, but she was trying to find romance for her and putting words in her mouth. It was a great disappointment for Mark and he began to send Adele angry letters. Finally, I told both Melody and her mother that I didn't want my son to be upset and that I thought it best that they should not contact each other anymore. It was another setback, but I was sure that more incredible things were about to take place—and sure enough, they did.

Michele and Dan would come and get Mark either on a Saturday or Sunday and take him to their house while I caught up on my rest. Sometimes they'd take him wading in the lake where they lived, and other times they'd help him try to ride a bike. Mark loved to go over there and looked forward to it all week. I remember that once Michele called me up and said, "Guess what, Mark can ride a two-wheel bike." I was thrilled. I had bought him a tricycle—a big one like senior citizens use. Bicycling was my only exercise and now Mark could ride with me. It was so amazing that he could ride a bike, but yet he couldn't walk unaided. Everyone would be somewhat surprised when he got off the bike, then wait for me and put his hand on my shoulder to balance himself, then walk that stiff walk.

Soon, a year had gone by since Mark had come home. His progress was wonderful. I could see my son coming back into his own, slowly but surely. His face was almost free of its grimace and every day he was looking more like his old self. His weight was finally normal, he was riding a bike and he was walking with a little less stiffness, and often without the help of someone's shoulder. The physical therapists had continued to clock him and count his steps and he was now able to walk from the beginning of the hallway to the end. He didn't do it very fast, but he did it. And at the pool, when Mark began walking in the water, my son-in-law had suggested that he swim like he used to. So Mark tried, and within a couple of hours, with Dan's help and encouragement, he was able to do it. I'll never forget that day. A short time later he was able to swim the length of the pool underwater, and I took a picture of him doing it to mark the accomplishment.

It was extremely rewarding to see my son getting better. Living with the new Mark was an incredibly interesting experience. I thank God for Drs. Stone and Farrow who clued me in on what to expect. They told me whatever tendencies a person had before suffering a brain injury would be magnified after his or her accident. For example, if someone were prone to bouts of depression, he or she would become twice as depressed afterwards. In Mark's case, he had always been a positive, pleasant person—always joking and enjoying life. Now I found that Mark's jokes were twice as frequent as they had been in the past. Before the accident, I used to compare his humor to Robin Williams, who always fits the joke to the occasion. Now, he sounded more like Tom Green, since he had no way of stopping whatever was in his mind from coming out of his mouth. It made for some interesting situations. Most of the time I was laughing for a good part of the day, but there were also plenty of occasions where his humor wasn't so appropriate and I would feel embarrassed and ashamed.

There was a bar next to the gym where Mark worked out. He had never been much of a drinker. In fact, I can't recall ever seeing him drink, and when he'd gone out in the past he was always the designated driver. But one day he walked into the bar after his workout and asked for a "vodka martini—shaken, not stirred"—as though he were James Bond. The bartender, not knowing who Mark was or what had happened to him, replied, "I think you've had one too many already." Anyway, when Mark heard this he thought it was funny, and after that he made a habit of stopping there everyday and saying the same thing. It took almost a month before someone told the bartender, "He's not drunk. He's that Navy SEAL who was in the skydiving accident."

His dentist, who was a friend of my daughter and son-in-law, took care of Mark's dental work. Once as Mark was coming out to the reception area, he told the people in the waiting room "Don't go in there! Look what happened to me when I was in there."

Mark could never pass a place that had a bell without ringing it. One time he wanted to visit Camp Walden, the summer camp he had gone to as a child. I called the owner and found that he was still running the camp after all those years. He was very gracious and said that we could come to visit, so we went the next day, arriving at around ten in the morning. Mark was thrilled to see the place that he had been familiar with as a child. I was in the office talking with one of the staff members when we heard a bell ringing outside. The whole camp turned out to find Mark standing beside the bell, laughing. I heard someone ask, "Who's that man ringing the bell? It's only supposed to ring at mealtime." Reluctantly, I said, "That person belongs to me."

Since he still had trouble with his short-term memory, Mark would repeat a joke about twenty-five times. His favorite was taken from the movie *Airplane...Surely you can't be serious. I am serious, and don't call me Shirley.* He was a child in many ways and I felt like he had to be protected, since I never knew what he was going to do, and he'd do everything on the spur of the moment. I always had to be on my toes. One day as I was driving, he saw someone with a surfboard on top of their car and wanted me to follow them. "Mark," I told him, "They could be going all the way to the ocean and we live in Michigan." He laughed when he realized the impracticality of what he'd asked me to do.

When I said it was incredible to live with him, I was including the fact that it was also a joyful experience to see him progress in his recovery, even if it continued to go slowly. My worry was that the more improvement he made, the more independent he'd become, which would be fine except for the fact that, because his brain was slower than his body, or sometimes vice-versa, I didn't know what to expect from one minute to the next.

Going to a restaurant proved to be interesting, as well. Mark had forgotten all manners, which made for a lot of laughs whenever we'd go out with my daughter and her husband and their children. The kids thought it was funny to see their uncle do all the things that they were told not to do. He would eat with his hands, since it was easier for him, or laugh with a mouthful of food which would ultimately go flying across the table. Finally, Michele suggested that I take him to quieter restaurants and teach him how to behave in public. I did, and his behavior slowly improved.

Mark was easy to influence. If I was angry at someone, he'd get angry at that person, too. Once there were signs posted all over town concerning a school that was to be torn down. Although this school was closed, there were a lot of people who wanted to preserve the building. The signs read: **SAVE OUR SCHOOL** and many of our neighbors had this sign in their yards. One day my daughter came over and said, "In my opinion that building should be torn down. It's dangerous for the children and they're going to have to do it eventually." Mark was there when Michele said this, and a short while later he grabbed his cane, went for a walk and began knocking down all these signs. He kept doing it until someone came out and said, "Hey! What are you doing to my sign?" Mark's response was to knock it down, at which the man told him he was going to call the police. When they arrived, the officer recognized Mark from the gym. "Hey, don't knock those down," he called. But Mark laughed, raised his cane and said, "You're going to have to catch me first." Then both of them started to laugh because he couldn't even walk without the aid of his cane. When he came home I had to give him a talking-to about the situation and tell him that he had to respect other people's opinions, even if they were different than ours.

If we were in a retail store and the phone rang, Mark would pick it up and begin to talk. It was tedious to constantly remind him not to do this. Some of the store owners would laugh, while others weren't too happy about it. Still, he went about his merry way, doing all these little things that he thought were funny. If he were in an elevator, Mark would always talk to everyone in it. Then he'd put his head against the wall and say, "Awe, good wall. Nice wall," just as he had when he'd first recovered from his vegetative state and had begun moving around. It made him look a little goofy now, and I tried to get him off of that bit. But it was hard to get Mark off of anything.

It was difficult to take him to the movies, too. He still had trouble swallowing and would make loud noises in trying to do so. He'd say anything he wanted, unaware of the others who were trying to watch the film. I remember a funny incident that happened when we went to see *Titanic*. I had pointed out to Mark that the woman who played the mother in the movie used to be married to Clint Eastwood, an actor of whom Mark was very fond, and that I'd heard that she had taken him for a lot of money. So when she came on in her next scene, Mark yelled out, "That's the bitch that divorced Clint Eastwood!" I wanted to slide down in my seat and pretend that I wasn't there. I felt despair, because he was so different from how he was before the accident.

Gradually, however, all these strange actions subsided until there came a point at which Mark began to take his recovery into his own hands. Suddenly he took his condition very seriously and worked excruciatingly hard at getting better. His disposition was still wonderful for the most part, but from time to time someone would trigger a fit of anger in him. This would only last for about five minutes though, and I knew that it would be followed by an obligatory, "I'm sorry," which would be followed by long moments of complete awareness of where he was and what was happening.

One good thing was that he remembered every moment of his past, and I was so thankful that he could remember all the good times he'd had in life, and even the bad times. Everything is an experience worth preserving. His short-term memory was improving, too. He started remembering what day it was, and made a point to keep it in mind. He became aware of what month it was, as well. Then he worked on remembering the names of different people he'd meet, which was the hardest thing for him. I had never been good with names myself and when he'd ask me who someone was, there were plenty of times where I couldn't help him. We'd sit and try to recall the name together until we'd finally start laughing at our lack of memory.

Mark continued to get publicity from the local television and newspapers, which was helpful because the locals came to recognize him, and would understand why he often behaved in odd ways, and everyone did what they could to help him. The gym where he worked out also had a body-building competition each year, and the owner asked Mark and I to attend. During the event, the owner pointed Mark out and told his story and the crowd gave him a standing ovation. Mark loved it. He always fed off of people's affection.

Unfortunately, our relationship with that gym was not destined to last much longer. Over the course of the next several months, Mark's condition really started to improve. He was walking a lot and he'd even started to run a little. At that time I got on the computer and wrote to the television show *Extra* and told them everything that my son had been through. To my surprise, they called me and asked if they could come to Petoskey and do a feature on him. This was national television and I was excited for my son. An *Extra* director and cameraman came to the house and began interviewing Mark, then myself and Michele. Then they went into town and tried to go to all the places where Mark would go. They went to his physical therapy office and took some pictures of Linda and Mark during his physical therapy session. Then they got some footage of Mark riding his bike. Unfortunately, when they talked about going to the gym, the cameraman said that they were running over and wouldn't have time to shoot anything there. I asked him to change his mind, stressing the role the gym had played in my son's recovery. But he insisted that it wasn't possible and said that even if we did shoot something, he'd have to cut it out when he edited. I had a feeling that the omission of the gym from the show would make for hard feelings, but little did I know that it would cause such tremendous resentment.

The show aired and they did a fabulous job in producing the piece. It wasn't very long, only about five minutes, but the reporter talked about Mark and his accident, then showed the clips and interviews they had done here in Petoskey. They also showed a clip of him jumping with The neuro-psychiatrist. The piece ended with Mark saying that he would never quit striving for a complete recovery.

After the show aired, it was clear that there was a lot of resentment at the gym. The owner, whom I had believed was my friend, told me that Mark was being disruptive, that he was trying to lift weights that were too heavy for him and that he was scaring the other customers by making strange noises while he practiced his speech therapy in front of the mirror, something he was supposed to do in order to see how words were formed. Instead of telling the people what Mark had been through and why he was doing this, the owner took exception to the action. She went on to tell me that I had to have a wake-up call, that my son had a brain injury, and that she had been told by at least thirty people that he was loud and behaving strangely. I was hurt, but I knew then that I could no longer leave my son there alone.

After that, Mark had to go to the gym with his personal trainer, and that was only twice a week. I later found out that the owner of the gym had been yelling at Mark quite frequently, and scolding him instead of quietly explaining what he was doing wrong. I had been told by his doctor that negativity would make Mark angry, and indeed he did respond to this woman's anger with anger of his own. When I tried to explain to her what a brain injury could do to a person, she blew me off by saying that she knew all about brain injuries and that I ought to face the fact that perhaps my son would never get better. That was the last straw for me. I couldn't leave him someplace where he wasn't wanted, or where seemingly everything he did was wrong—compared to his first year there when he could do no wrong. I decided never to let him go there again.

Mark didn't understand what was going on, the politics of it all. He had loved to walk down to the gym, which was convenient for me, too, but I was willing to drive as many miles as it would take to get him out of that atmosphere. I took him to the local racquetball club, where they had a gym, as well. There was a trainer there named Scott Conti who worked with Mark and became his friend. Everyone at this new gym was wonderful to Mark. They included him in their post-workout get-togethers and I often thanked God that everything had worked out the way it did. Mark and Scott understood each other and became inseparable. Sometimes things have a way of working out—often at the time when it seems like nothing will—and so it was with this new gym and Mark's new friend.

The experience also made me realize that there were some people from whom I had to protect my son.

As far as I was concerned, Mark was a hero, although no one else knew the full extent of his courage except his sisters and me. The fatigue that follows a brain injury is so great that the sufferer has to actually force him or her self to make every single move. And to see this man trying so hard with the workouts and the physical therapy and the speech therapy was amazing. It was an effort that I couldn't explain to anyone who wasn't seeing it on a daily basis.

TRAVELS WITH MARK

In the spring of 2000 Mark had quite an adventure when his friend Bill invited him to go to Florida to stay with some of their friends. They were to stay at Larry's house in Vero Beach and would fish and surf at Sebastion inlet and Monster hole, a surf spot that they all frequented during their youth. Often they would be gone for two weeks at a time. I didn't have any objections to this trip since the year before they went to their high school reunion in Ft. Lauderdale and all went so well. Little did I know that Bill thought that his best friend was not improving fast enough and he was certain it was because he lived with me and was treated like a child. Bill wanted to push him to do better so he decided he was going to get Mark to walk better and faster in the two weeks he would have with him in Florida. Of course his motivation came from his great friendship and love for Mark, but as it turned out he was not considering the complexity of a brain injury.

He came to get Mark the day before the trip and I drove them to the Traverse city airport early the next morning. As we said good-bye, Bill told me not to expect any phone calls from them because they would be traveling by car through Florida. I should have guessed then, that Bill was on a mission. I told him to call Jacki who lives in Ft. Lauderdale if they needed any thing and off they went, Mark smiling and walking next to Bill, with his usual stiffened gait. I drove back the two hours to Petoskey feeling happy that he was going to be with people his age, but of course I was worried about his memory loss and confusion causing problems for him.

I did not hear from them for ten days and was told by my daughters that no news is good news. Finally, Bill called me telling me he was at the beach. Mark was taking a walk but he wanted me to know every thing was fine and they would be going to Ft. Lauderdale where Mark would go see his sister for a couple days. Bill would visit his uncle and then pick him up for the return trip. He told me that they walked every day together and Mark could now jump down from a table and could walk better than before he left. I was not surprised because in physical therapy Mark had been jumping from the steps, but then would forget how until his therapist would remind him to do it again. It was not until years of the same routine that it finally became part of him, but if it made him happy to think this was all new, it was fine with me. I told him I wanted to talk to Mark as soon as he arrived at his sister's house. I was so happy to talk to him when he called two days later. He said he was having a good time and Bill was a jerk, but he was laughing so I thought it was all in good fun. Jacki mentioned that he was tired and was sleeping a lot. I was anxious to have him come home.

I went to get Mark at the Traverse City airport. Bill had put him on the plane in Detroit to travel alone because he had to go back to his job as a pilot for Northwest. I saw Mark coming towards me with his back pack and his hands in his pockets trying desperately to walk as normal as possible. His eyes were so wide opened that I was scared he was going to have a seizure. His face was sun-burned and as he said hello he seemed in a rush to get to the car. When he flopped down on the car seat I said, "What's going on?" He said, "Bill is a jerk and I punched him, and I do not want to talk about it". He then fell asleep and stayed asleep for the rest of the trip. As soon as we were home he laid down on the couch and I could not wake him up to go to his bed that night. He had a class the next day at the college, and I told him not to go but he insisted

An hour after I dropped him off I received a call from the school office telling me to pick him up because he was not feeling well. When I picked him up and took him home, he went straight to the couch again and was there for the next two weeks. He would get up just to eat, and began to tell me little by little of what took place while he was gone.

Apparently, Bill had him up early every morning, he called it zero hour, he made him walk very fast and gave him the boot camp treatment. Bill did not understand that in new territory Mark loses all confidence and gets very disturbed due to his lack of balance. When they all went fishing and of course had a few beers, they did not pay much attention to him. One of those days, he took off for a walk on the beach but did not know how to get back. It was a hot 99 degrees, and after hours of looking for him and waiting for him to return, they called beach security and got a helicopter to find him. That explained his sun burn. They all had a good laugh after the fact but Bill did not know that the result of pushing him when he was under both the mental and physical pressure of being in a new place, was not improvement, but fear and anger. Mark told me that Bill tried to make him go in the ocean at night without a life jacket and wanted him to feel bad about not being like the Mark he once was. Mark's reaction was to finally punch him in the face and fight him. To Bill's surprise, they rolled on the ground until he said to him, "Mark friends don't hit friends." When I got what I thought was most of the story I called Bill and got terribly angry at him. We argued about it all and he knew I was furious. But his last words broke my heart when he said, "I wanted my friend back." I think I reached him when I told him I wanted my son back too, but you have to accept him the way he is day by day. I could never stay mad at Bill, he was a part of our life and of course Mark could not either. Bill is now a dad and understands better about what it is to be a parent. He is still Mark's best-friend.

As I had promised, we returned to California. We went to see the ocean and the place where he used to live. We went to his old surf hangout, Wind and Sea, where you could only reach the ocean by climbing down a hill. Mark was so disappointed that he couldn't climb down that I said, "Okay, let's try it anyway," and the two of us tried to climb down backwards. I guess we must have looked pretty comical. Halfway down, when we couldn't go any further, we began our customary laughing at ourselves; an old woman helping a man who could hardly walk go downhill toward the ocean. Finally two young surfers took pity on us and helped us get down.

So there we were, right next to the Pacific. We walked to the sea, and when Mark took off his shoes and waded into the ocean I was so happy that I wanted to cry. There were surfers skimming the waves and I knew that it had to have been hard for him to watch them, but I felt in my heart that one day he would be out there again. I told him so—and I really think that he believed me. He had already made so much progress in other areas of his life that he probably figured *Why not?*

We ran into an old buddy of his, a surfer who had gained local fame by killing sharks from his surfboard. He was thrilled to see that Mark had made it back to his old beach, and Mark was glad to see him, too. We stayed a little while longer, then we headed back uphill to the place where we had parked the car. Going back up was just as bad as getting down. Because Mark was better at this than I was, he pushed me until we had nearly reached the top, at which point and as had happened before, someone helped us.

While we were in California we visited Mark's old friend, Scott. We also went to the gym where Mark had worked out after he was released from the hospital. And we went to see Dr. Stone and had lunch with the neuro-psychiatrist.

I had dropped Mark off in front of the restaurant and went to park the car. When I returned, he was talking to a man who was obviously an alcoholic from the streets. Mark's left hand was shaking quite a bit at that time and the street bum said to him, "My God, man, you need a drink real bad." Mark said, "I just quit. Why don't you quit too?" and the man said, "Not if it's going to make me shake like that." I thought it funny that they were talking like they were old friends.

I had a rental car which allowed us to go everywhere that Mark wanted to go. One of his old friends that we visited was a man named Lenny, with whom he'd worked with before he became a SEAL. Lenny was in the business of producing videos. I asked if he could put a video together for Mark, one that would include skydiving clips and some home videos from Guam. As it turned out, Lenny was happy to do this for us free of charge and the video turned out well.

I always wondered what Mark's future would be like. The question of whether or not he would be able to hold a job was always in the back of my mind. Finally, an answer to that question came. His friend Foot in California had once suggested to me that Mark should be making speeches, but I couldn't foresee how it would come about. However, in the fall of 1999, while Mark was still in college, he was asked to make a speech in front of other physically challenged people. To my amazement, when he got up on stage, he came alive. He was witty and articulate and I knew immediately that this was going to be his future

When we returned to Michigan, Mark made more speeches. He was asked to speak for a wonderful program, *Decision to Action*, which was a program set up for troubled teens. The first speech was good, although he was a little hard to understand, but he managed to make the audience laugh. The kids loved him, I think because they knew he was speaking from the heart and they responded to him because of this. From there on, though, he made more and more speeches and was better and more humorous each time. Before going on stage he had Michele write what he wanted to say on index cards. He'd go through these cards on stage, then show a series of videos. The first one was of the training involved in becoming a Navy SEAL. The second was of some of the skydiving he'd done with the Leap Frogs, and the third video was the clip from *Extra*. Then he'd close with some extemporaneous speaking and have the crowd join him in saying three times, "I will never quit!" His speeches were so well received and he was a different person when he was in front of an audience-in short, he was *on*. It was so great for me to see him do this. He was the pre-accident Mark. I remember the doctor telling me that whatever was learned would never be lost, so it gave me hope in that he was successful with his speeches, and thus may be able to do well in things beyond that.

I wrote to one of his officers on the SEAL teams, explained what Mark was doing, and asked him if he could get us some paraphernalia to hand out to people after the speeches. He managed to send us quite a bit of material, along with pictures of the Leap Frogs. After that, Mark would give each kid an autographed picture upon the conclusion of his speech. It was wonderful to see the kids interact with him and to hear them repeat, "I will never quit."

My niece Daniele invited us to go to France in April of 2001, and after some thought I took her up on it. I was a little leery at first because Mark still wasn't walking all that well. But it *did* sound exciting so we went-and it was the best thing we ever did. Two days before we arrived, Daniele called me saying that she was friends with the Secretary of the Elysee and his wife, both of whom worked for President Chirac. The Secretary's daughter had been in one of my niece's films, a film that had enjoyed huge success in France just a month before our visit. Shortly before the spring Daniele's friend had gone to see her at her home and she showed her the video I had sent of Mark. She was so impressed and moved by his story, that she told her husband and President Chirac.

As a result of this, Daniele called us and said, "Bring something for Mark to wear because we've been invited to have lunch at the Elysee with the Secretary and his wife, and maybe Mark will get a chance to meet the President." We were thrilled and very honored. We got Mark a suit and tie for the occasion. Shortly after we arrived in Paris, we found ourselves waiting in our hotel room for Daniele, her husband Albert, and daughter Caroline to come and pick us up. They were very late in getting there, and when we got to the Elysee, it took quite a while to pass through security. When we were finally ushered in to the main building, we learned that President Chirac was not able to wait for us and had left. However, he had told the Secretary that he was particularly interested in Mark's story since it reminded him of a similar challenge he'd had in his youth, and that he regretted not having been able to shake Mark's hand.

During our subsequent tour of the Elysee, we went into a magnificent office regally decorated with a desk that had belonged to Louis XIV. I was taking a few pictures and marveling at the splendor of it all when, out of the corner of my eye, I saw Mark sitting at this incredibly beautiful desk, with his feet kicked up on it just as though he were at home. "Mark, please don't!" I protested, but he thought it was funny. As I was trying to stop him, the wife of the Secretary (Madame DeVillepin) said to me, "Oh, no...no. Don't worry, My husband does that all the time." I wasn't sure if she was just saying that to make me feel better, but she did convince me to take a picture of Mark sitting with his feet propped up on the President's desk, the desk that once belonged to King Louis XIV.

After that, we had some pictures taken of us with the guards, and of this magnificent building. We then had the most wonderful lunch with Daniel's friends who could not have been any nicer to us or more interested in Mark and how he was doing. All this was such an honor and I felt so happy for my son. It was an adventure that we would never forget. I do wish we had met President Chirac, but just the idea that he was willing to meet my son was an honor in itself.

After we returned to the States, I received a letter in the mail from Madame DeVillepin. Enclosed was a newspaper clipping that showed her husband sitting at the President's desk with his feet propped up on it. Above the picture she had written in pen, "See I told you, he does it too."

From Paris we went to Daniele and Albert's new house in St Tropez. They were wonderful to Mark and he was excited to see his cousins Caroline and Christopher, who both had newborn babies. We spent a delightful few days with them in St. Tropez, and when we went to the beach and Mark saw all the beautiful topless girls sunbathing he said, "I guess this is why I came out of my coma." We all laughed. There wasn't one day that Mark didn't say something hilarious. Each morning he'd go up to the front desk of the hotel where we were staying in Paris, and in his broken French he'd say to the girl, "Vous etes jolie mademoiselle," which means you are beautiful. It always brought a smile and a "Merci, monsieur." And he took the American saying *It's all good* and translated it into *Tout est bon.*

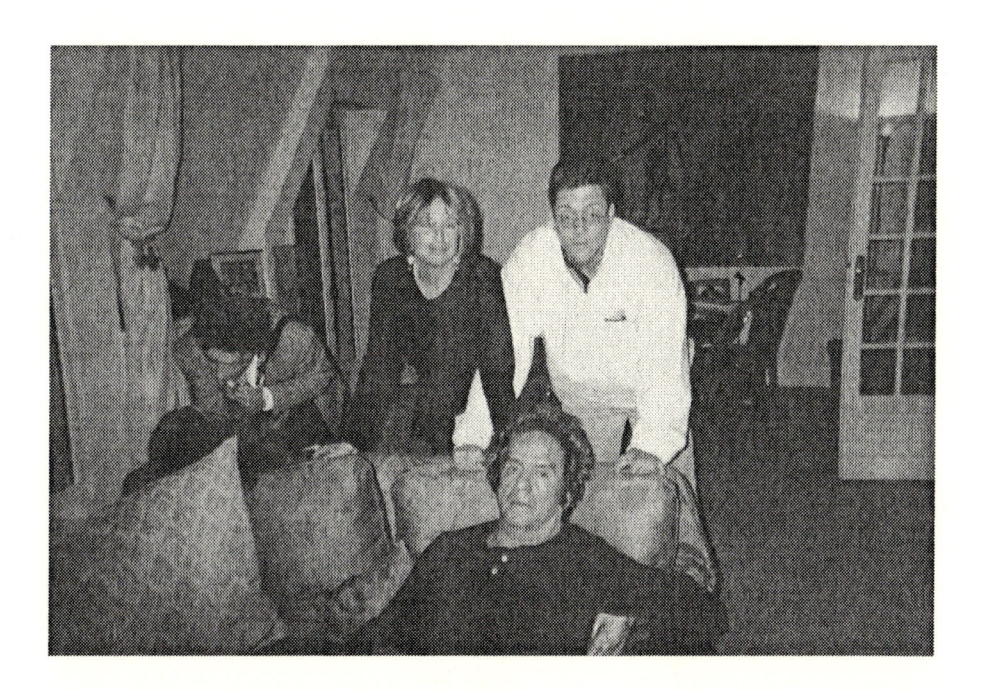

While we were at the airport, there were five or six people in wheelchairs who were waiting to board their plane. Mark didn't want to use his because he could walk if he pushed the luggage cart for support. His physical therapists had been trying to teach him to skip to work on his balance, and so he was practicing down the airport corridor. Suddenly he got it—just as he was passing people in their wheelchairs he yelled out "Look! I can skip!" He was laughing and I was happy that he was happy. But at the same time I felt so sorry that this had happened in front of people who might never even walk again.

After a short wait we boarded our plane. Mark had enjoyed the time with his French family as much as I and I was so grateful for their hospitality. Even after we returned to the States, I felt warmed by their love and understanding.

LITTLE VICTORIES

Mark was still using a cane, but he didn't want one like everyone else had, so he got one of those long wooden sticks that look like a snake, and made him look a little like Moses. About ten times a day he'd throw the stick on the ground as Moses did and we'd all watch as if it would indeed turn into a snake. One day as we entered Michele's house, she took the cane and said, "That's it. No more." Michele always seemed to know when he was relying too much on either the walker or the cane and when she said he could walk without it, she was always right with her instinct. She could see this better than me since I lived with him and was a bit overprotective, and he would listen to her and trusted her judgment. Just as with every other time he had to give up some device that was helping him, Mark bore that look of fear, but reluctantly he said, "Okay" and started walking without his cane from that moment on.

Everything took time and time was the foundation that he had to build on. His broken bones had healed in expedient fashion, but the healing of the brain was and is an ongoing process. The thing that was so incredible though, was witnessing the progress. Each time he achieved a new goal or did something for the first time it was a victory to him and to all of us who cared about him. His life had become a series of little victories.

There were times when things were not so pleasant too. One day as Mark was taking a shower, there was a knock at the door. I opened it and there stood a policeman along with another man in a suit who said he was from the FBI and told me he wanted to ask Mark a few questions. At first I wondered if it was one of his friends pulling some hoax, particularly since a lot of the SEALS do go into the FBI after their naval careers are over. When Mark suddenly arrived in the living room, straight from the shower, stark naked and laughing, it was their turn to be surprised.

I told Mark to go get some clothes on and when he returned a short while later wearing a pair of pants, the FBI man said to him, "We're here because you've been sending threatening emails." I couldn't believe what I was hearing but it turned out that Mark had been talking to a woman online in the brain injury chat room who was afraid that her husband was going to divorce her and take her kids away. Knowing that Mark was a Navy SEAL, she had asked him to scare her husband a little which Mark apparently, fancying himself in the role of savior, had promptly done. At all events, he sent an email to this woman's husband, saying that he was going to come after him if he didn't leave her alone.

Just as Mark had always felt like Superman, he'd always felt like a savior as well. I remember that when he was a boy, there had been a little girl in the neighborhood who was retarded and the other kids would tease her. Mark had always come to her defense. She'd arrive at our door with accounts of how the other kids had insulted her and Mark would go find them and say that they'd have to fight him if they didn't knock it off. So it was no surprise to me that he was trying to protect someone now.

There were many states between us and where this man lived, and I told the FBI man that even if he had taken Mark's threats seriously, there would be no way he could get to this man without me driving him there and obviously, I wasn't about to do that. After talking to us the FBI officer understood the situation and simply explained to Mark that he couldn't write emails of that nature any more. In the end, it turned out that there was a legitimate reason for the FBI to be concerned, but not with Mark so much as the woman who had him send the threatening email. It seems that her husband thought she was actually trying to hire someone to kill him. After the men left, we never heard from them again, but all this shook me up a little. It was disturbing to know that someone could easily convince Mark that he should do something that was clearly criminal in order to save a damsel in distress. I cautioned him that, because the people in the chat room also had brain injuries, he had to be careful.

Then there was another incident, although not on the scale of the previous one, where Mark and his friend Eric, a twenty year old with cerebral palsy, went to a local restaurant, La Senorita for dinner. Eric's mother drove them down there, and I was to pick them up when it was time for them to come home. I was wondering how this would go, but I felt it was time to take a chance and let him do something on his own. An hour and a half later I went to get them and they were standing outside the restaurant, both laughing hysterically. I asked them what was going on and Mark said that they had asked them to leave the restaurant. What happened was that Mark had decided that his young friend should have a girlfriend, so he proceeded to go to each waitress saying, "Do you like my friend? I think he'd like to go out with you." If she didn't respond, he'd go to the next one saying the same thing. This went on until the manager told him to quit doing it saying the girls were busy working. I don't know what happened after that, but between the two of them, they had aggravated the manager to the point where he told them they had to wait outside. It seemed I had left them alone there just long enough to eat and get into trouble. We had a talk about behavior in a restaurant on the way home.

On another occasion Mark was to meet Eric in front of the gym where he used to work out, and from there they were going to walk to the movie theatre. I had never told Mark exactly why I had found a new gym for him to use because there was no sense in hurting his feelings so it was understandable that, when Eric didn't arrive on time, he should go into the familiar door of the gym and ring their bell like he had done many times before. The owner, the same woman who had been so unpleasant before, apparently took one look at Mark and called the police, something she frequently did, apparently, when anything displeased her.

I knew nothing about this, of course, until Mark came home and began telling me that she had asked him to leave. He was understandably confused and, when I received a call from an unidentified man, telling me that Mark was no longer welcome there, I assumed it was from someone from the gym and told him to go to hell before slamming down the phone. Needless to say, it was quite unlike me to respond this way, but I was quite upset.

A short time later, two police officers appeared at our front door and I discovered that I had told one of them, not the gym employee off, on the phone and hung up. Once he understood that I had had no idea who I was talking to, however, he assured me that Mark had not done anything out of the way. Later, I learned that the owner of the gym had rubbed a lot of people the wrong way. But the important result of all this was that I began to watch my son more closely, trying to keep negative people out of his life. I felt rightly or wrongly, as though he still needed protection, even though he was beginning to become more aware of reality and respond less and less like an innocent child.

DON'T YOU EVER DIE!

Three years after his accident, Mark decided that he wanted to be called Marcus. He felt that his life had changed so dramatically, that he wanted a new name as well. Whenever I feel sad, I think back to the beginning of this incredible journey and just how far we have come. I am amazed at my family's strength throughout these difficult years. Mark's attitude about life, his life, is so positive and hopeful, despite the early loss of his father, the loss of his twin babies, and the loss of his life as he knew it before May 17th 1997. At the end of his most recent speech, I heard him tell the audience that if it weren't for his troubles, he would be bored. On any given day he can be found at the gym helping friends and giving advice about exercise and diet, always with a joke, a laugh, and a smile.

Now I can say that I've found my son again (even though he changed his name from Mark to Marcus.) He's beginning his new life and there's more hope than I would ever have thought possible. People love him for his good nature and his perseverance over all the obstacles he's had in his life. I want everyone to know that Mark has seen the light at the end of the tunnel. He is now in terrific shape, strong and muscular and fit, and he takes care of his own diet and training. He goes to the gym by himself every day, and once a week he gets his friend Scott to help him train. He can jump rope, run, swim, and when we go bike riding I can no longer keep up with him. He always tries very hard to fix his stiff appearing gait when he walks and seems to be more relaxed jogging than walking. Adam and Linda from Tim Bondy Physical Therapy are his buddies and they work with him "to the max."

His brain injury will always be a factor in his life. He experiences heightened fatigue and when very tired, his progress seems to falter. His speech is less clear and thoughts seem difficult to come forward, but he knows he has a relentless will to recover as fully as possible, and once rested, he is back to full force. His judgment is constantly improving. The injury to the frontal lobe of the brain caused him to speak impulsively without thinking or considering the ramifications. I thank God that most of his uncontrolled utterances were humorous to us and most other people. Thankfully, you can tell him not to do something and he won't do it again, unless he truly forgets.

Mark still goes into the TBI chat room and onto their discussion board. He has many brain-injured friends there from all walks of life, and it's good for him to have these people who can empathize with him, and he with them. Anyone who knows a person with a brain injury should visit this chat room, where people like my son can compare notes and give hope to one another. When *Marcus* is in the chat room he makes others laugh, and sometimes he makes them angry. They can make him angry too, but mostly they give one another such good advice and help, each with their personal experiences and progress.

It's so hard to understand someone with a brain injury; you really have to love a person to endure all the ups and downs. Their ailment is unlike any other because it affects every part of the body, every part of a life. It takes a very strong person to overcome this, someone like Mark. One minute in the life of an individual can change them forever, set aside everything they've accomplished in life and force them to start all over again. I have learned so much from my son and his life, and I want to convey the transcending power of hope, to others who are entering this new world.

Like other mothers, I'm always afraid that I'm not going to be here when my son needs me, but I know that he also has two sisters, family and friends to give him the help and support he needs. That is what a brain-injured person needs more than anything else.

Each year millions of people suffer brain injuries: from a fall, from aneurysms, strokes and from car accidents. Many of these people will never recover and as a result, many lives are altered. The recovery may be long, but inch by inch they can come back toward some reality. If I have learned one thing from all of this it's to be more patient and understanding of other people who have any kind of affliction. Many of the people who visit the discussion board complain of not being understood even by their own families.

My son was in the elite forces of the Navy SEALs. Now he's in the elite force of survivors. I listen to *Marcus'* friends on the TBI discussion board, and to me, all of them are heroes. Their chat names are KiwiDan, Sagasha, Scar, Zapp, Dr. Rick, Mia, Bobby, Bluebear, Linda, Bobby, California-caregiver, Louise, Jetagirl, Debbie, Becky, Rita, another Mark, Laura, RichardF, Jordan, KidJoe, JoyH, Bev, Amy, Meeskite, ShortStuff, BlueStar, and Dee, Maya and *Marcus,* who chats using the name Underfrog. I could go on and on with the names of people who visit that room, and all of them could tell you a different story. Every day new people come into the room. When they come in, many sounding weak with fear because their loved-ones are in a coma, we tell them what we've been through, and try to give them hope and encouragement. We all pray for one another.

To live on the edge was part of his being and that has not changed, only the challenges have changed. He does not dwell on the things he can no longer do, but he still reaches for the moon.

After six years of re-learning, last summer Mark decided he would do a triathlon in Coronado, California that he had done many years before with his SEAL buddies. He would not be dissuaded and began training very hard, biking, running and swimming. After six weeks of this, he was making great improvements in his endurance and strength, despite his wheezy breathing, balance difficulties, and awkward gait. Friends encouraged him, Michele and others helped him train, and it seemed that he might actually reach his goal to participate in the race. But it was not meant to be.

Two weeks before we were to leave for Coronado, during a training ride, Mark lost his balance and fell. He had learned to protect his left hand and arm that had been so badly damaged in his accident, so he did not use it to break his fall to his left side. And so, he fell on and broke his left hip. I thought his spirit would be broken along with his hip, and it seemed so for the next few months. He had wanted so much to participate and finish the triathlon. I was hoping to finish this memoir with his triumph. Instead, Mark faced surgery and rehabilitation again. I put my writing on hold for a while, as my heart ached for him to be well again.

Less than a year later Mark is now doing very well, and again training with enthusiasm. I am ending my writing here, knowing that reaching for the moon is a never ending story, so mine will go on. My son's laughter, unbreakable spirit, and thrill for new challenges will keep us both living life to the fullest extent. He lives by the words that he recites to himself when passing by a mirror, "Don't you ever die, a quitter never wins and a winner never quits." Those words are always followed by the SEAL motto, "The only easy day was yesterday," and when he says goodbye to someone it's always, "Hasta la vista, baby."

This summer he had another little victory when he got back on water skis for the first time since the accident. He loves life, he loves to make speeches and he longs to make them in front of a large crowd. He wants to relay his message, *Never give up and never quit. The only easy day was yesterday.*

The only time I really saw Marcus depressed was during the days of the 9/11 tragedy. He knew well that he wouldn't hear from his SEAL friends as much as he had in the past and he was so sad that he couldn't go with them. There was nothing I could say, for in my heart I was in shock—like the rest of the country—and in a way I felt relieved that Marcus couldn't go. These mixed feelings were so depressing for me.

I recently turned seventy-seven and I have learned so much in the last few years. I now know that love is a great catalyst for accomplishment, and that nothing is impossible. I have watched my son reach new goals and I have witnessed that he has as much fun striving for these goals as he does when he completes them. I don't know what the future will bring—I can only leave it in the hands of God and thank him for what he did for us. I'm grateful for the people who helped him: the doctors, the Navy SEALs, Mark's ex-wife Eva, his physical therapists and the people at the gym where he now goes—where he doesn't have to be ashamed of being himself. I thank my daughters and their families: Michele and Dan and their children, Griffin, Ryder, Boone and Wes: and Jackie and Nicholas, and my family in France: Danièle, Albert, Caroline and Christopher. Whenever I felt defeated or discouraged, my family and friends were there for me. I thank all of Mark's friends, those that he had as a boy and those that he met later in his life, especially Bill, who was and still is like a brother to him. But mostly I thank Mark himself for being so strong and for loving life.

This certainly was a journey that had its ups and downs, and there will be many more on the road ahead, but I look at it now and I can only say, "My God, he did it! He's a survivor!" His spirit and thrill for new challenges will keep him living his life to the fullest extent. He truly does live by the words that he recites passing by a mirror, :Don't you ever die!" and "A quitter never wins and a winner never quits". But it's his SEAL motto that is forever etched in his brain that lets him know that daily challenges are his life, because *The only easy day was yesterday.*

My Own Words-When I Left the Green Room

Well, I think I will begin as best I can recall which after a brain injury is very limited. My memories begin with my Mom wheeling me in a wheelchair to have some sort of test. I was informed later that it was a CAT scan, MRI or something. I do know that there was some sort of shot involved and I was in a tube like enclosure with a white light. I thought when I died that I was supposed to head down some sort of tube towards a white light but this was ridiculous. Besides, it made a terrible hellish pounding on the sides of the tunnel. I remember my Mom who I assumed was a nurse that changed my sheets, fed me and did other assorted tasks. I referred to her as Mrs. Colburn which is what I heard everyone else calling her. I remember listening to music, McCartney, Sting, James Taylor from inside of my padded cell. Whenever there was that kind of music, I felt happy and safe. I got to know exactly which song was the final song on a tape and that the tape would need to be turned over. This was the only grasp of reality that I had any control over.

I also remember a weird tube like thing that stuck out of my stomach. That horrified me. I also remember seeing myself in the bathroom mirror, this skinny guy with a long plastic tube staring right back at me. He had this nutty look in his cocked eyes, like one of the guys I used to see in movies about concentration camps. Man was I pissed. Is that me?

I recall hiding in my padded cell from Don (the physical therapy guy) cause I knew he was there to get me out of my safe warm padded cell. I seem to remember going to physical therapy from my cell with Andy (the chief of the LEAPFROGS). I thought he could understand me cause I visited him in the hospital when he was injured. We rode the stationary bike, or he was there to help me struggle through it.

I remember very well asking my Mom when I would get my tummy tube removed. Dr. Stone appeared one day in my padded cell and said he would be back on Monday to remove it. Well, Monday came and no Dr. Stone. My mother told me that he was a very busy man and to just be patient. Sure enough he arrived one day. He stated that he was late because he had to talk to the doctor who put the tube in to find out exactly the right procedure to remove the tube. He then proceeded to pull it out of my tummy and it bled pretty bad. Stone smiled a dry smile and said that he would send me the bill for the sheets.

It was finally gone. Now I was under the impression that this nightmare was over. It was just like the military saying, "training is never over". I later was informed by Don (the P.T.guy) that there was a tiny spring that was permanently maneuvered into my vein from my leg to my heart to prevent blood clots.

I guess I am the "six million dollar man".

978-0-595-35588-4
0-595-35588-9